Russia and the Long Transition from
Capitalism to Socialism

# RUSSIA AND THE LONG TRANSITION FROM CAPITALISM TO SOCIALISM

Samir Amin

MONTHLY REVIEW PRESS
*New York*

Library of Congress Cataloging-in-Publication data available from
the publisher.
—

Names: Amin, Samir.
Title: Russia and the long transition from capitalism to socialism / Samir
  Amin.
Description: New York : Monthly Review Press, 2016. | Includes
  bibliographical references and index.
Identifiers: LCCN 2015049045| ISBN 9781583676011 (paperback) | ISBN
  9781583676028 (hardcover) | ISBN 9781583676035 (e-book trade) | ISBN
  9781583676042 (e-book institution)
Subjects: LCSH: Russia--Social conditions. | Soviet Union--Social
conditions.
  | Russia--Economic conditions. | Soviet Union--Economic conditions. |
  Social change--Russia--History. | Social change--Soviet Union--History. |
  Capitalism--Russia--History. | Socialism--Soviet Union--History. | Soviet
  Union--History--Revolution, 1917-1921--Influence. | Soviet
  Union--History--1985-1991.
Classification: LCC HN523 .A68 2016 | DDC 306.0947--dc23 LC record available
  at http://lccn.loc.gov/2015049045


Typeset in Dante Monotype

Monthly Review Press
146 West 29th Street, Suite 6W
New York, New York 10001

monthlyreview.org


5 4 3 2 1

# Contents

THE ESSAYS COLLECTED IN THIS BOOK CHALLENGE the currently fashionable views that are promoted by the media clergy, through their use of propaganda, on behalf of the financial aristocracy. Russia, as was the Czarist Empire and the Soviet Union, is continually presented as a horribly despotic and aggressive nation against which the civilized peoples of Europe have always had to, and still must, protect themselves. Today protection is available thanks to the military power of the United States and NATO. These cookie-cutter judgments will be revisited in the conclusion of this book.

The various essays here focus on complementary aspects of a very different interpretation of Russian history, one that is viewed in the long run, within the context of a global history that places Russia in the world system at each of the successive stages of its development.

Although these essays were written at different moments between 1990 and 2015, they all contribute to shaping an image of Russia that is quite different from the one that is disseminated in the propaganda of the Western countries. It is only by using a scientifically accurate analysis of history (and it is up to the reader to judge the quality of my effort) that it is possible to envisage the various prospects available to the peoples of Russia and the former Soviet Union and the conditions of their reemergence in the world of tomorrow.

# 1. Russia in the Global System: Geography or History?

The double collapse of Sovietism as a social project distinct from capitalism and the USSR (now Russia) calls into question all the theories that have been put forward both regarding the capitalism/socialism conflict and the analysis of the positions and functions of the different countries and regions in the world system. These two approaches—the first giving priority to history, the second to geography, are often exclusive of one another. In the tradition of historical Marxism, and particularly in its predominant version in the former USSR, the only great problem of the contemporary world recognized as worthy of scientific treatment was that of the passage of capitalism to socialism. As from Lenin, a theory of revolution and socialist construction was gradually formulated, which is summarized in the following points:

(i)     capitalism must finally be overturned throughout the world through the class struggle conducted by the proletariat;

(ii)   the socialist revolution has started in certain countries (Russia first, later in China) rather than in others because they constituted, for various reasons, the "weak links" in the chain of world capitalism;

(iii)  in those countries, the construction of socialism is possible in spite of their late development;

(iv)  the transition of capitalism to socialism will therefore evolve in, and through, the competition between the two state systems, some of which have become socialist, the others having (provisionally) remained capitalist.

In this type of analysis, history—which governs the social and political particularities that constitute the different societies in the modern world (including those of the "weak links")—plays the key role, to the point that the geography of the world system, in which the various positions and functions of these societies are determined, is entirely subordinated to history. Of course, the reversal of history, overturning the "irreversible socialism" on behalf of capitalism, must question the whole theory of the transition to socialism and its construction.

Geography, however, takes on another dimension in, for example, an analysis of the movement of modern history that is inspired by the fundamental principle of what one can call, to be brief, the "world system" approach: what happens at the level of the whole (the world system) controls the evolution of the parts that compose it. The roles played by the Russian Empire and by the USSR would therefore be explained by the evolution of the world system, and this is what makes it possible to understand the collapse of the Soviet project. Just as the extremists among the historical Marxists only know the class struggle through history, an extremist interpretation of the world system approach is possible, one that virtually eliminates class struggle because it is incapable of changing the course imposed on it by the evolution of the system as a whole.

It is useful to mention here that theories about the specificity of Eurasia and its particular place in the world system preceded the formulation of the world system approach by several decades. In the 1920s, Russian historians (Nikolai Trubetzkoy and others) had put forward such proposals, which were then forgotten by official Soviet conformism, but they were resuscitated in recent years. The theses developed in an article by Andrei Fursov in *Review* recall the theory of the Eurasian specificity in certain aspects and distinguishes it from others. I would be in favor of a synthesis of the two types of analysis, particularly as concerns the Russian-Soviet case. Having already defended such an approach in more general terms, I believe such a synthesis to be enriching for Marxism.

Between the years 1000 and 1500, the world system was clearly composed of three main blocs of advanced societies, China, India, and the Middle East, to which can be added a fourth, Europe, whose development was extremely rapid. It was in this last region, which had been marginal until the year 1000, that the qualitative transformations of all kinds crystallized and inaugurated capitalism. Between Europe and eastern Asia—from the Polish frontiers to Mongolia—stretched the Eurasian landmass, whose position in the global system of the period largely depended on the way these four regions articulated what can be called the ancient world system (precapitalist tributary social system, if my definition of these social systems is accepted).

It seems impossible to give a convincing picture of the birth of capitalism without taking into consideration the two sets of questions concerning (i) the dynamics of the local transformations in response to the challenges confronted by these societies, particularly the dynamics of social struggles, and (ii) the articulation of these dynamics in the evolution of the ancient world system seen as a whole, in particular the transformation of the roles of the different regions that composed the ancient world system and, therefore, the functions of the Eurasian region.

If we are to take the global viewpoint into consideration and thus relativize the regional realities, we must recognize that the great majority of the civilized population of the ancient world was concentrated in the two Asian blocs, China and India.

Moreover, what is striking is the regularity of growth of these two blocs; their population of some 50 million inhabitants grew to 330 and 200 million in 1800 and 450 and 300 million in 1850, respectively. These extraordinary increases compare with the stagnation of the Middle East, precisely from the Hellenistic period. The population of the latter probably attained its maximum—50 million—at this time and then declined almost regularly, stabilizing at around 35 million on the eve of the industrial revolution and European penetration. (It should be recalled that the population of Egypt had been 10 to 14 million inhabitants at certain epochs of the pharaonic age, but it fell to 2 million in 1800. The decline of Mesopotamia and Syria was of the same order.) A comparison should also be made with the stagnation of barbarous Europe until the year 1000. The population went from 20 million two centuries before the Christian era to probably less than 30 million toward the year 1000 before exploding to 180 million inhabitants in 1800 and 200 million in 1850.

It is then easy to understand that Europe, when it became aware of itself, became obsessed with the idea of entering into relationships, if not conquering, this fabulous Orient. Until late in the eighteenth century, the Chinese Empire was, for the Europeans, the supreme point of reference, the society that was the most civilized, the best administered, and its technologies that were the finest and most effective (Étiemble, 1972). The power of the Chinese Empire was such that it was only from the end of the nineteenth century that anyone dared to attack it. In contrast, India, which was more fragile, had already been conquered and its colonization played a decisive role in British progress. Fascination with the Far East was the main impulse of such European initiatives. However, the discovery and conquest of the Americas absorbed European energies for three centuries. The function of Eurasia must be seen in this perspective.

The Middle East, considered by some as the region that was the heir of Hellenism (a synthesis of five cultures: Egypt, Mesopotamia, Syria-Phoenicia, Greece-Anatolia, Iran) constituted the third pole of advanced civilization.

The intense trade between these three poles thus affected the dynamic of the ancient world. These "silk routes," as they are called, crossed the southern region of Eurasia, from the Caspian Sea to China, to the south of the Kazakh steppe, from Tian Shan to Mongolia (Amin, 1991).

Nevertheless, the relative stagnation of the Middle East pole (for reasons that are not relevant to this study) ended in a gradual decline of its foreign trade. There were at least two important consequences. The first was that Europe became aware, thanks to the Crusades, that the Middle East was not a rich region to conquer for itself, but the zone to be crossed, or bypassed, to reach the really interesting regions of Asia. The second was that China and India diverted their sights from the west to the east, constituting the peripheries that really interested them in Korea, Japan, Vietnam, and Southeast Asia. The two eastern poles did not actively search for relations with the Middle East and still less with Europe. The initiative was therefore taken by the Europeans. The Eurasian landmass and the ocean were the main competing passages enabling the Europeans to enter Asia.

Europe was, as has been already said, marginal until toward the year 1000. Like Africa—which remained marginal after the year 1000—Europe was a region in which the people were not really settled, or constituted, in tributary state societies. But this poor periphery of the ancient system suddenly took off within a particular structure that combined a peripheral feudal tributary form (the fragmentation of powers) and a European universalism of Roman Christianity. During the progress of this system, which was to conclude by Europe becoming the center of the capitalist and industrial world in the nineteenth century, it is possible to distinguish successive periods that, in turn, define the roles that Eurasia was to play in the accelerated dynamism of the system.

The Crusades (1100–1250) were the first stage in this rapid evolution. Western (Frankish) Europe then sought to break the monopoly of the Middle East, the obligatory (and expensive) passage for its relationships with eastern Asia. This monopoly was in fact shared between Orthodox Christian Byzantium and the Islamic Arab-Persian Caliphate. The Crusades were directed against both of these two adversaries and not only the Muslim infidel, as is so often thought. However, finally expelled from the region, the Europeans tried other ways of overcoming this obstacle.

The Crusades accelerated the decline of the Middle East, reinforcing still further the lack of interest of the Chinese in the West. In fact, the Crusades facilitated the "Turkization" of the Middle East: the increased transfer of powers to Turcoman military tribes, who prepared the simultaneous destruction of Byzantium and the Caliphate, which were succeeded, from 1450–1500, by the Ottoman Empire.

Furthermore, the Crusades enriched the Italian towns, giving them the monopoly over the navigation in the Mediterranean and prepared their active role in seeking ways to bypass the Middle East. It is interesting to note that two major routes were opened up by Italians: Marco Polo, who crossed the Russo-Mongol Eurasian landmass and, two centuries later, Christopher Columbus, who crossed the Atlantic Ocean.

Eurasia entered into history at that time, between 1250 and 1500, during the course of the second phase of this history. Its entry marginalized the ancient silk routes that linked the Middle East to China and to India by the southern part of central Asia, to the benefit of a direct Europe-China liaison, passing further to the north, through the Eurasia of the Genghis Khan Empire (this was exactly the route of Marco Polo). In turn, it opened the secular struggle for the control of Eurasia between the Russians of the forest and the Turko-Mongols of the steppes. The formation of the Muscovite state had several impressive stages: liberation from the Mongol yoke, increased expansion through Siberia, and military conquest of the southern steppes up to the Black, Caspian, and Aral Seas, the Caucasus mountain range, and finally south-central Asia and Transcaucasia.

This history bequeathed Eurasia with some special characteristics that strongly differentiated it from the European formations as well as those of China. It did not, as is said rather superficially, become (or remain) "half-Asian" (the expression obviously being in a pejorative sense). In fact it is too far away from the Chinese model to be so described. But nor did Eurasia become constituted into a densely populated, homogenous state as gradually happened in Europe, with its absolute monarchies and then with its modern bourgeois nation-states. The occupation of such a large area weakened such characteristics, in spite of the desire of St. Petersburg, as from 1700, to imitate European absolutism. Also, in the Russian Empire the relationship between the Russians and the Turko-Mongol peoples of the steppes was not the same as the relationship developed by the Europeans during their colonization of other nations. The Russian Empire did not exploit the work of the Turko-Mongols, as the Europeans did in their colonies; it was a political power (Russian) that controlled the spaces occupied by both peoples. This was, in a way, perpetuated in the Soviet Union, where the Russians dominated in political and cultural terms but did not economically exploit the others (on the contrary, the flow of wealth went from Russia to central Asia). It was the media that popularized and confused these profoundly different systems by superficially calling them both empires (S.Amin, 1992b).

Eurasia did not, however, play the role of a passageway linking Europe to China except for a short period, between 1250 and 1500, at a stage when Europe did not yet have sufficient absorption capacity to bestow Eurasia with the same financial brilliance for transport as would be placed on maritime commerce. From 1500, in fact, the Atlantic/Indian Ocean route replaced the long continental crossing. And this was not only a geographical substitution. Heading west, the Europeans "discovered" America, conquered it, and transformed it into a periphery of their budding capitalism, a destiny that Eurasia had escaped and would not have been possible to impose upon it. At the same time, the Europeans had also learned how to colonize Asian countries (transforming them into peripheries of world capitalism), starting with India, the Dutch East Indies, and the Philippines, then Africa and the Middle East, which was done in different ways from those invented during the Russian expansion into Asia.

The maritime route re-marginalized Eurasia from 1500 until 1900, and continued even after that. The Russians responded to the challenge in an original and, in many aspects, brilliant way. Fursov remarked that in 1517 the monk Philotheus had proclaimed Moscow to be the third Rome. This observation is worth bearing in mind because, as it was made so shortly after the maritime route had been opened, it gave Russia an alternative perspective, an exclusive role in history. There were some, like Nikolai Berdyaev, for example, who believed that Soviet communism pursued this aim of the messianic role for Russia in advancing the progress of all humanity.

Russia built itself up from then on, making an effective synthesis of retreating into itself and opening to the West. The former task, that of a self-centered construction, was therefore in complete opposition to the peripherization of world capitalism. There was no equivalent to this except for the self-centered construction that the United States had pursued from its independence until 1914, or even until 1941.

So there were two large spaces that organized themselves as self-centered continents, obeying one sole political power. There have been no others, except for China, since 1950. Nevertheless, one cannot but note the mediocre results obtained by Russia/USSR compared with the brilliant ones of the United States. There is a conventional explanation for this contrast that contains a lot of truth: the advantage of the United States not having a feudal heritage (an argument reinforced by pointing out that New England was not constituted as a periphery of capitalism). But it is necessary to add that by being "isolated" on the American continent, the United States was free from the vicissitudes of European politics and had only one adversary—Mexico—which was too weak to be anything other than prey, and half of its territory was taken. On the other hand, Russia was not able to avoid the European conflicts and had to deal with rivals from Western and Central Europe: Russia was thus invaded by the armies of Napoleon, had to endure the affront of the Crimean War, and was then twice more invaded in 1914 and 1941.

This continual interference in the history of Russia and that of Europe was at least in part the result of the Russian—then Soviet—choice not to close itself up in Eurasia but to remain, or become, as modern, that is, as European, as possible. This was the choice of the St. Petersburg Empire, symbolized by the two-headed eagle, one of whose heads looked toward the West. But it was also the choice of the USSR, which infused its ideology into the traditions of the European workers' movement. The USSR's total rejection of Slavophile and Eurasian ideologies, which had always survived in the Russian Empire, despite its official pro-Western option, is an obvious consequence of this.

The Russian Revolution does not seem to have constituted a less important phenomenon that would hardly influence the course of history once the Soviet parenthesis was closed. There is little other convincing explanation for this revolution other than by simultaneously involving history (the new contradictions introduced by capitalism) and geography (the position of Russia in the capitalist economic world).

Capitalism certainly introduced a new challenge to the whole of humanity, to the peoples of its advanced centers, and to those of its backward peripheries. On this essential point,

I remain completely Marxist. By this I mean that capitalism cannot continue indefinitely as permanent accumulation and the exponential growth that it entails will end up in certain death for humanity.

Capitalism itself is ripe to be overtaken by another form of civilization, one more advanced and necessary, through the leap in people's capacities of action that accumulation has enabled (and which is a parenthesis in history) and by the ethical and cultural maturation that will accompany it.

The question that the Russians posed in 1917 is neither artificial nor is it the odd product of their so-called messianic impulses or the particular circumstances of their country. It is a question that is now posed to the whole of humankind.

The only questions that have now to be answered are the following:

(i) Why did this need to overtake capitalism so strongly manifest itself here, in Russia, and then in China, and not in the advanced capitalist centers?

(ii) Why did the USSR fail to change this need into a lever of irresistible progressive transformation?

In response to the first question, the geography of the world system certainly played a decisive role. The Leninist formulation of the "weak link" is a first effort to explain what, in that sense, Mao generalized for the peripheries of the system in the theory of the continuous revolution by stages, starting from New Democracy. It is an explanation that takes into consideration the polarization produced by the world expansion of capitalism, even though it does it imperfectly, as can be seen today. The Russia that believed to be "starting the world revolution" was not a peripheral country. It had the self-centered structure of a center, but a backward one, which explained the violence of the social conflicts that took place. The second great revolution—that of China—developed in the only large country that was not well and truly "peripherized" as was Latin America, the Middle East, India, and Southeast Asia. China had never been colonized. Instead of the well-known Chinese Marxist formula, a country that is "half-feudal, half-colonial," perhaps "three-quarters tributary, one-quarter colonial" is more correct, while the other peripheries are "one-quarter tributary (or feudal) and three-quarters colonial."

The second question requires a response that starts by challenging the theory of the "socialist transition" as has been sketched above. This transition is inexact, as it does not adequately address both the history and the geography of capitalism. This theory is based on an underestimation of the (geographical) polarization of the centers and peripheries, and it does not recognize that it is due not to particular historical circumstances, the "natural" tendency of capitalist expansion being to homogenize the world, but to the immanent results of this very expansion. The socialist transition theory therefore does not see that the revolt of the peoples who are victims of this development, which is necessarily unequal, has to continue as long as capitalism exists. It is also based on the hypothesis that the new (socialist) mode of production does not develop within the old (capitalist) one, but beside it, in the countries having broken with capitalism. This hypothesis should be replaced with one where, in the same way that capitalism first developed within feudalism before breaking out of it, the long transition of world capitalism to world socialism is defined by the internal conflict of all the societies in the system between the trends and forces of the reproduction of capitalistic relations and the (anti-systemic) trends and forces, whose logic has other aspirations—those, precisely, that can be defined as socialism. Although it is not the place here to develop these new theses concerning the long transition, it is necessary to mention them because they explain the reasons for the failure of Soviet Russia.

We may conclude by posing the questions that can throw light on the debate concerning not only Russia but also the world system.

The Soviet failure is not due to Russia, nor to the nineteenth century, nor to—as Fursov suggests—the pre–St. Petersburg Moscovite period. For Russia, as for any other country, going back in history makes no sense. It is more a case of freeing oneself from this superficial kind of exercise and looking at the future from the viewpoint of an analysis of the present and its new features and comparing this with the past.

How to get out of capitalism and go beyond it remains the central question for the Russians, the Chinese, and all the other peoples of the world. If the thesis of the long transition that is sketched here is accepted, the immediate step is to deal with the challenge that confronts us all: building up a multipolar world that makes possible the maximum development of anti-systemic forces. This implies for the Russians and for the other peoples of Eurasia (formerly USSR) not an illusory capitalist development but the reconstruction of a society capable of going beyond it. A series of problems arising from this study should consider whether the Russians or the Chinese will be able to do this in the immediate future, or whether other peoples will do it more easily.

## REFERENCES

Amin, Samir, "The Ancient World System versus the Modern Capitalist World System," *Review*, 14, (Spring/Summer 1991), 349–86.

———. "Capitalisme et Système-monde." *Sociologie et Sociétés*. 24, no. 2, (Autumn 1992), pp. 181–202.

———. "Le défi de la mondialisation," *Actuel Marx*, in English, *RIPE* (*Review of International Political Economy*), 1992.

Étiemble, Rene, *L'Europe chinoise*, (Paris: Gallimard, 1972).

Trubetskoy, N. S., *Letters and Notes of Trubetskoy*, (The Hague: Mouton, 1975).

Trubetzkoy, N. S., *The Legacy of Genghis Khan and Other Essays on Russia's Identity*, Anatoly Liberman, ed., (Ann Arbor: Michigan Slavic Publications, 1991).

Vernadsky, George, *A History of Russia*, (New Haven: Yale University Press, 1961).

# 2. The Czarist Empire versus the Colonial Empires

The image of the Czarist Empire conveyed by currently fashionable views is that of a despotic system that expanded geographically by conquering non-Russian peoples of Europe and Asia and subjecting them to an odious colonial regime. A "general theory" of the formation, expansion, and inevitable collapse of "empires" has been put forward by Paul Kennedy,[1] whose ahistorical and non-scientific method I do not share. I shall return to a critique of this work in the conclusion.

This chapter establishes and defends two theses. The first concerns the formation of Greater Russia (which included Russians, Belarusians, and Ukrainians in the same state), which was similar to the formation of modern France and Great Britain. The second concerns the expansion of the empire from the borders of Germany to those of China. This expansion was different from the construction of the Western colonial empires, whether British, French, or others.

The media compelled all of us to follow closely both the Scottish referendum of September 2014 and the conflict between Russia and Ukraine, which increased its momentum in the spring of 2014. We all heard two opposing stories: the unity of Great Britain must be protected in the interest of the English and Scottish people, but the Scots freely chose, through a democratic vote, to remain in the Union. On the other hand, we are told that the independence of Ukraine, freely chosen by the Ukrainian people, is being threatened by the Great Russian expansionist aims of the dictator Putin. Let us look at these facts that are presented to us as incontrovertibly obvious for a good-faith observer.

### The Formation of Great Britain

Great Britain (the United Kingdom) unites four nations (these are the terms used by David Cameron): England, Scotland, Wales, and Northern Ireland. These four nations must continue to live together in a single state because it is in their interest to do so. Being in favor of Scottish independence was thus presented as irrational, emotional, and without any serious foundation. Independence would have brought nothing good to the Scots.

These are some of the common arguments we heard: the petroleum resources on which Scotland depends will be exhausted sooner than many believe. Moreover, it is foreign international companies that actually carry out the exploitation of those resources (the implication being that they could leave in the event of a vote in favor of independence). The Scots are anxious to maintain some social benefits in education and health that the Westminster Parliament abolished when it lent its support to the neoliberal dogmas adopted and imposed by the European Union. David Cameron promised to take these demands into account by enlarging the local powers (of each of the United Kingdom's four nations).

Of course, the final decision is not within Cameron's power, but in that of the Westminster Parliament and Brussels. An independent Scotland would have to renegotiate its membership in the European Union, if it would so desire, and the process would be painful, long, and difficult. We are not told why that would be the case. After all, if an independent Scotland were to maintain the major European laws in force (which the supporters of independence did not question), it is difficult to see why it could not have been immediately recognized as a member of the European Union. It is also difficult to see why this process of joining the European Union would have been as painful as that to which countries from afar have been subjected (Lithuania or Bulgaria, for example), many having been forced to reform their economic and social systems completely. The media even dared to say, with a straight face, that an independent Scotland would no longer be able to export its whiskey to England, or elsewhere!

In this debate, there was one great silence: no one made the comparison to Norway, a country with a population comparable to Scotland's, and one that even shares the same petroleum resources of the North Sea. Norway, moreover, has chosen to remain outside the European Union and has benefited from this choice with a margin of autonomy that allows it to protect—if it so wishes—its social policies. Norway has, nevertheless, chosen to align itself more and more with the liberal economic policies of the European Union (we will not discuss the impact of this choice here, which is negative, in my opinion).

Behind the debate on the interests of Scots lie different interpretations of history. The Scots, just as the Welsh and the

Irish, were Celts (and spoke Celtic languages) and fought the English (Anglo-Saxons) and subsequently the Anglo-Norman invaders of the British Isles. The Scots were ultimately defeated and integrated into what was a "Greater England." The arrogance of the English monarchy and aristocracy in relation to the defeated Scots was not erased from their memory, even if, it seems, this page were turned later, perhaps only after the Second World War, with the triumph of the Labour Party and the social advances that triumph made possible.

The Scots, nevertheless, were truly integrated: they permanently lost the use of their language, just like the Occitans or Bretons in France. It is pointless to welcome these changes (Anglicization or Francization) or deplore them: it is a historical and irreversible fact. The Scots benefited from the union because they were able to emigrate easily to the industrial cities of England, the colonies and dominions, and the United States. They provided a good number of officers for the British army to train troops recruited in the colonies (a little like the Corsicans in France). But above all, and this appears to be the strongest argument, Scotland and England were formed into a single modern, completely unified capitalist economy (just as were northern France and Occitania). There are undoubtedly more Scots (or people of Scottish ancestry, even if distant) who live and work in England than in their country of origin. In that way, Scotland cannot be compared with Norway.

And yet, despite this profound integration, which is, let us acknowledge, no longer discriminatory, the Scots like to think of themselves as distinct from the English. The English monarchy and aristocracy invented the Anglican version of the "Reformation," i.e., Catholicism without the Pope (who was replaced by the King of England). The Scots chose a different path, the Calvinist reformed churches. The difference no longer has importance today, but it was important in the nineteenth century and even in the first half of the twentieth century.

The official interpretation of history, widely accepted by the peoples concerned, does not hesitate to describe the union of the four nations into the contemporary United Kingdom as "positive overall." This is what David Cameron and the British leaders of all the major parties in the UK tirelessly repeated. But this is also the opinion expressed by half of Scottish voters. This view could be taken, at the price of fracturing a difficult-to-heal public opinion, even if the pro-independence half made an irrational choice (contrary to its interests) out of romanticism. What is not said is that exceptional means were systematically used to convince voters to vote against independence. To describe these means as blackmail or even as intellectual terrorism would not be overdoing it. The election, even if it was formally completely free and transparent, is not in itself proof of the legitimacy, credibility, and permanence of the choice it ratified.

The history of the formation and continuity of the United Kingdom is thus a beautiful history stained only by its failure in southern Ireland (Eire). The conquest of Ireland by the arrogant English lords, who grabbed the land and reduced the Irish peasants to a condition close to serfdom, with its disastrous demographic effects (repeated famines, massive emigration, depopulation), was nothing but a particularly brutal form of colonization. The Irish people resisted by hanging onto their Catholicism and ultimately reconquered their independence in 1922. But it remains the case that colonization led to the imposition, to this day, of the dominant use of the English language. Eire today is part of the European Union, whose dependence on British capitalism is attenuated only by its dependence on other major partners in the contemporary liberal world economy.

In summary, then, the suggested conclusion is that the differences inherited from history by the four nations of the United Kingdom do not dictate the breakup of Great Britain. The history of British capitalism is painted in shades of rose, not black.

### The Formation of Russia and the Soviet Union

The media discourse on Greater Russia—the former Russian Empire of the Czars—and the Soviet Union takes on a completely different tone. In this case, we are told that we must come to a different conclusion: the differences are such that there was no other solution than to break up the formerly unified entity into distinct and independent states. But let us look a little more closely. The development of Greater Russia within the framework of the Czarist Empire, followed by its profound transformation during the construction of the Soviet Union, was, as we are supposed to understand it, a black history, governed by the continual exercise of extreme violence alone.

This view needs to be challenged. The unification of three Slavic peoples (Great Russian, Ukrainian, and Belarusian) by the czars of Moscow, followed by Russian expansion to the Baltic in the west and to Siberia, the Transcaucasus, and Central Asia to the east and south, was no more violent and less respectful of the identity of the peoples affected than was the development of historical capitalism in the Atlantic West (and, within this context, of British capitalism) and its colonial expansion. The comparison even favors Russia, as these three examples illustrate:

(1) The unification of the three "Russian" peoples (Great Russian, Ukrainian, and Belarusian) was certainly made through military conquest by the czars, as was the construction of France or Great Britain through military conquest by their kings. This political unification was the vector through which the Russian language was imposed—"naturally"—on local dialects. The latter were, moreover, considerably closer to one another than were, for example, the *"langue d'Oïl"* and the *"langue d'Oc"* in France, English, and the Celtic languages, or the Italian dialects in Sicily and Venice. To present linguistic Russification as a horror imposed by violence alone, as opposed to a supposedly tranquil expansion of French, English, or Italian, is to ignore historical reality. Again, the nature of these linguistic expansions and whether they were a long-term enrichment or cultural impoverishment is beyond the scope of this chapter. The point is that all of these linguistic expansions are historical facts of the same kind.

The Russians did not eliminate the Ukrainian and Belarusian ("feudal") landowners; they were integrated into the same system that dominated Great Russia. The serfs and (after 1865) the free peasants of Ukraine and Belorussia were not treated differently than those of Great Russia; they were treated just as poorly.

The Bolsheviks' communist ideology painted the history of czarism in shades of black for good class reasons. Consequently, the Soviet Union recognized the differences (which were denied in the "civilized" West) and created distinct republics. What is more, to fight the danger of being accused of Great Russian chauvinism, the Soviets gave these republics boundaries that largely exceeded those that would have been drawn by a strict ethnolinguistic definition. One territory, such as Russian Crimea, could be transferred to another republic (in this case to Ukraine) without a problem. Novorossiya ("New Russia"—the Donetsk region), distinct from Malaia Rossiia ("Small Russia"—Ukraine), could be entrusted to Kiev's administration rather than Moscow's without causing any problems. The Bolsheviks had not imagined that these boundaries would become the borders of independent states.

(2) The Russians conquered the Baltic countries during the same time period the English settled Ireland. The Russians did not commit any horrors comparable to those of the English. They respected the rights of the local landowning elites (in this case, Baltic barons of German origin) and did not discriminate against the local subjects of the Czar, who were certainly poorly treated, just like the serfs of Great Russia. The Russian Baltic countries certainly experienced nothing comparable to the savage dispossession of the Irish people in Northern Ireland, who were chased out by the invasion of the Orangemen. Later, the Soviets restored the fundamental rights of the Baltic republics, permitting the use of their own languages and the promotion of their own cultures.

(3) The expansion of the Czarist Empire beyond the Slavic regions is not comparable to the colonial conquest by the countries of Western capitalism. The violence carried out by the "civilized" countries in their colonies is unparalleled. It amounted to accumulation by dispossession of entire peoples, with no hesitation about resorting to straightforward extermination, that is, genocide, if necessary (the extermination of the North American Indians and the Australian Aborigines by the English are but two examples) or, alternatively, brutal control by a colonial government (as was done in India and throughout Africa and Southeast Asia). The czars, precisely because their system was not yet a capitalist one, conquered territories without dispossessing the inhabitants. Some of

the conquered peoples were integrated into the empire and were Russified to varying degrees, notably through using the Russian language and often forgetting their own. This was the case with many of the Turco-Mongolian minorities, though they retained their religion, be it Muslim, Buddhist, or Shamanist. Others preserved their national and linguistic identity—the Transcaucasus and Central Asia south of Kazakhstan. None of these peoples were exterminated like the North American Indians or Australian Aborigines. The brutal autocratic administration of the conquered territories and Russian arrogance prevent us from painting this history in shades of rose. But it remains less black than was the behavior of the English in Ireland (though not in Scotland), India, North America, or that of the French in Algeria. The Bolsheviks painted this history in shades of black, and always for the same good reasons of class.

The Soviet system brought changes for the better. It gave these republics, regions, and autonomous districts, established over huge territories, the right to their cultural and linguistic expression, which had been despised by the czarist government. The United States, Canada, and Australia never did this with their Indigenous peoples and are certainly not ready to do so now. The Soviet government did much more: it established a system to transfer capital from the rich regions of the Union (western Russia, Ukraine, Belorussia, later the Baltic countries) to the developing regions of the east and south. It standardized the wage system and social rights throughout the entire territory of the union, something the Western powers never did with their colonies, of course. In other words, the Soviets invented an authentic development assistance, which presents a stark contrast with the false development assistance of the so-called donor countries of today.

There was no inherent reason that this system, with an economy that was completely integrated at the level of the union, had to disintegrate. There was no objective necessity that had to lead to the breakup of the union into independent states, which were sometimes even in conflict with one another. Western media chatter about the "necessary end of empires" does not hold water. Yet the USSR indeed broke apart, which needs to be explained.

### The Breakup of the USSR: Inevitability or Conjuncture Created by Recent History?

The peoples of the Soviet Union did not choose independence. There was no electoral process, neither in Russia nor elsewhere in the union, prior to the declarations of independence, which were proclaimed by those in power, who themselves had not really been elected. The ruling classes of the republics, above all in Russia, bear complete responsibility for the union's dissolution. What's important is to know why they made this choice when they made it. The leaders of the central Asian republics did not really want to separate from Russia. It was the latter that presented them with a *fait accompli*: the dissolution of the union.

Yeltsin and Gorbachev, who rallied to the idea of completely and immediately reestablishing liberal capitalism through "shock therapy," wanted to get rid of the burdensome republics of central Asia and the Transcaucasus (which benefited, in the Soviet Union, from capital transfers from Russia). Europe took it upon itself to force the independence of the Baltic republics, which were immediately annexed to the European Union. In Russia and Ukraine, the same oligarchs stemming from the Soviet *nomenklatura* seized both absolute political power and major assets from the large industrial complexes of the Soviet economy, which were privatized in haste for their exclusive benefit. It is these players who decided to separate into distinct states. The Western powers—the United States and Europe—are not responsible for the disaster at this initial stage. But they immediately understood the advantage they could gain from the disappearance of the union and then became active agents intervening in the two countries (Russia and Ukraine), stirring up hostility between their corrupt oligarchs.

Of course, the collapse is not solely the result of its immediate cause: the disastrous choice of the ruling classes in 1990–1991. The Soviet system had been rotten for at least two decades. The abandonment of the revolutionary democracy of 1917 in favor of an autocratic management by the new Soviet state capitalism is, in fact, the origin of the rigidity of the Brezhnev era, the rallying of the political ruling class to the capitalist perspective, and the ultimate disaster.

Although it has retained the neoliberal capitalist model for its internal economic management (in a "Jurassic Park" version, to use Aleksandr Buzgalin's expression), Putin's Russia has not been accepted by contemporary collective imperialism (the G7: United States, Europe, and Japan) as an equal partner. Washington and Brussels' objective is to destroy the Russian state (and the Ukrainian state), reducing them to regions subject to the expansion of the capitalism of the Western oligopolies. Putin became aware of this later, when the Western powers prepared, financed, and supported what can only be described as a Euro-fascist coup d'état in Kiev.

The question that is posed now is thus a new one: Will Putin break with economic neoliberalism to embark on, with and like others (China in particular), an authentic project of economic and social renaissance, the "Eurasian" alternative that he announced the intention of constructing? It must be understood, though, that this construction can move forward only if it knows how to "walk on two legs," that is, to pursue both an independent foreign policy and economic and social reconstruction.

## Double Standards?

By comparing the Scottish situation with that of Ukraine, we can only note the duplicity of the words and actions of the Western powers—indeed, they maintain a double standard. The same duplicity exists for a host of other issues that are beyond the scope of this chapter, but examples include how the West was for German unity, even though the annexed "Easterners" paid for this dearly, but against the unity of Yugoslavia, Iraq, and Syria. In reality, behind this appearance looms the one and only criterion that governs the choices of the governments of collective imperialism (United States, Europe, Japan): the viewpoint of dominant financial capital. But to see this clearly in their choices, we must proceed further in analyzing the system of contemporary capitalism.

## The State in Contemporary Capitalism

Why, and by what means, are these dominant policies used to strengthen the state in some places and destroy it elsewhere? The answer to this has three components:

(i) Since 1980, capitalist production has been involved in a qualitative transformation that can be summed up in this way: what we are seeing is the emergence of a globalized production system that is gradually being substituted for the earlier national production systems (which were autonomous and simultaneously aggressively open systems in the center and dominated systems, to varying degrees and in various forms, in the peripheries). These national production systems were articulated in a hierarchical world system (characterized, among other things, by the center/periphery contrast and the hierarchy of imperialist powers).

In the 1970s, Sweezy, Magdoff, and I had already advanced this thesis, which was formulated by André Gunder Frank and myself in a work published in 1978. We said that monopoly capitalism was entering a new age, characterized by the gradual—but rapid—dismantling of national production systems. The production of a growing number of market goods can no longer be defined by the label "Made in France" (or the Soviet Union or the United States), but becomes "Made in the World," because its manufacture is now broken into segments, located here and there throughout the world.

Recognizing this fact, now commonplace, does not imply that there is only one explanation of the major cause for the transformation in question. One explanation is the leap forward in the degree of centralization in the control of capital by the monopolies, which can be described as the move from the capitalism of monopolies to the capitalism of generalized monopolies. In fifteen years (between 1975 to 1990), a large number of these monopolies (or oligopolies) located in the countries of the dominant triad (United States, Europe, Japan) became capable of controlling all production activities in their own countries and in the entire world, reducing the entities involved, *de jure* or *de facto*, to subcontractors. Consequently, they have been able to siphon off a significant share of the surplus value produced by these subcontracted activities, which ends up increasing the rent of the dominant monopolies in the system. The information revolution, among other factors, provides the means that make possible the management of this globally dispersed production system. But these means are only implemented in response to a new objective need created by the leap forward in the centralized control of capital. For others, the means—the information revolution and the revolution in production technologies—are themselves the cause of the transformation in question.

The dismantling of national production systems, themselves the product of the long development of capitalism, involves almost every country in the world. In the centers (the triad), this dismantling can appear relatively slow and limited due to the weight of the inherited and still active system. But each day it advances a bit more. On the other hand, in the national production systems of the peripheries, which had made progress toward the construction of a modernized national industrial system (the Soviet Union, Eastern Europe, and, to a lesser degree, in scattered places in Asia, Africa, and Latin America), the aggression of capitalism of the generalized monopolies (through submission—voluntary or forced—to the so-called principles of globalized neoliberalism) is expressed by a violent, rapid, and total dismantling of the national systems in question and the transformation of local production activities into subcontracted activities. The rent of the generalized monopolies of the triad, the beneficiaries of this dismantling, becomes an imperialist rent. Viewed from the peripheries, this transformation can be described as a re-compradorization. This process has affected all countries from the former Eastern bloc (former Soviet Union and Eastern Europe) and all countries in the South. China alone is a partial exception.

The emergence of this globalized production system eliminates coherent "national development" policies (which are diverse and unequally effective), but it does not substitute a new coherence, which would be that of the globalized system. The reason for that is the absence of a globalized bourgeoisie and globalized state, to be examined later. Consequently, the globalized production system is incoherent by nature.

Another important consequence of this qualitative transformation of contemporary capitalism is the emergence of the collective imperialism of the triad, which takes the place of the historical national imperialisms of the United States, Great Britain, Japan, Germany, France, and a few others. Collective imperialism finds its *raison d'être* in the awareness by the bourgeoisie in the triad nations of the necessity for their joint management of the world and, in particular, the subjected, and yet to be subjected, societies of the peripheries.

(ii) Some draw two correlates from the thesis of the emergence of a globalized production system: the emergence of a globalized bourgeoisie and the emergence of a globalized state, both of which would find their objective foundation in this new production system. My interpretation of the current changes and crises leads me to reject these two correlates.

There is no globalized bourgeoisie (or dominant class) in the process of being formed, either on the world scale or in the countries of the imperialist triad. There is an increase in direct and portfolio investment flows from the triad (particularly major flows between the transatlantic partners). Nevertheless, based on a critical interpretation of the major empirical works that have been devoted to the subject, the fact that the centralization of control over the capital of the monopolies takes place within the nation-states of the triad (United States, each member of the European Union, Japan) much more than it does in the relations between the partners of the triad, or even between members of the European Union, should be emphasized. The bourgeoisie (or oligopolistic groups) are in competition within nations (and the national state manages this competition, in part at least) and between nations. Thus the German oligopolies (and the German state) took on the leadership of European affairs, not for the equal benefit of everyone, but first of all for their own benefit. At the level of the triad, it is obviously the bourgeoisie of the United States that leads the alliance, once again with an unequal distribution of the benefits.

The idea that the objective cause—the emergence of the globalized production system—entails *ipso facto* the emergence of a globalized dominant class is based on the underlying hypothesis that the system must be coherent. In reality, it is possible for it not to be coherent. In fact, it is not coherent and hence this chaotic system is not viable.

In the peripheries, the globalization of the production system occurs in conjunction with the replacement of the hegemonic blocs of earlier eras by a new hegemonic bloc dominated by the new comprador bourgeoisie, the exclusive beneficiary of the dismantling of the earlier systems (the means by which this transformation was produced are well known: the privatization of parts of the old dismantled system, the assets of which were sold at artificial prices incommensurate with their values). These new comprador bourgeoisie are not constitutive elements of a globalized bourgeoisie, but only subaltern allies of the bourgeoisie of the dominant triad.

Just as there is no globalized bourgeoisie in the process of formation, there is also no globalized state on the horizon. The major reason for this is that the current globalized system does not attenuate but actually accentuates conflict (either already visible or potential) between the societies of the triad and those of the rest of the world. Conflict here refers to conflicts between *societies* and, consequently, potential conflict between states. The advantage derived from the triad's dominant position (imperialist rent) allows the hegemonic bloc formed around the generalized monopolies to benefit from a legitimacy that is expressed, in turn, by the convergence of all major electoral parties, right and left, and their equal commitment to neoliberal economic policies and continual intervention in the affairs of the peripheries. On the other hand, the neocomprador bourgeoisie of the peripheries are neither legitimate nor credible in the eyes of their own people (because the policies they serve do not make it possible to "catch up," and most often lead to the impasse of lumpen development). Instability of current governments is thus the rule in this context.

Just as there is no globalized bourgeoisie even at the level of the triad or that of the European Union, there is also no globalized state at these levels. Instead, there is only an alliance of states. These states, in turn, willingly accept the hierarchy that allows that alliance to function: general leadership is taken on by Washington, and leadership in Europe is assumed by Berlin. The national state remains in place to serve globalization as it is. It is an active state because the spread of neoliberalism and the pursuit of external interventions require that it be so. We can thus understand that the weakening of this state by a possible breakup for any of a variety of reasons is not desirable for the capital of the generalized monopolies (hence the hostility to the Scottish cause examined above).

There is an idea circulating in postmodernist currents that contemporary capitalism no longer needs the state to manage the world economy and thus that the state system is in the process of withering away to the benefit of the emergence of civil society. To put it briefly, this is a naive thesis and one that is propagated by the dominant governments and the media clergy in their service. There is no capitalism without the state. Capitalist globalization could not be pursued without the interventions of the United States armed forces and the management of the dollar. Clearly, the armed forces and money are instruments of the state, not of the market.

But since there is no world state, the United States intends to fulfill this function. The societies of the triad consider this function to be legitimate; other societies do not. But what does that matter? The self-proclaimed "international community," that is, the G7 plus Saudi Arabia, which has surely become a democratic republic, does not recognize the legitimacy of the opinion of 85 percent of the world's population!

There is thus an asymmetry between the functions of the state in the dominant imperialist centers and those of the state in the subjected, or yet-to-be-subjected, peripheries. The state in the compradorized peripheries is inherently unstable and, consequently, a potential enemy, when it is not already one.

There are enemies with which the dominant imperialist powers have been forced to coexist—at least up until now. This is the case with China because it has rejected (until now) the neocomprador option and is pursuing its sovereign project of integrated and coherent national development. Russia became an enemy as soon as Putin refused to align politically with the triad and wanted to block the expansionist ambitions of the latter in Ukraine, even if he does not envision (or not yet?) leaving the rut of economic liberalism.

The great majority of comprador states in the South (that is, states in the service of their comprador bourgeoisies) are allies, not enemies—as long as each of these comprador states gives the appearance of being in charge of its country. But leaders in Washington, London, Berlin, and Paris know that these states are fragile. As soon as a popular movement of revolt—with or without a viable alternative strategy—threatens one of these states, the triad arrogates to itself the right to intervene. Intervention can even lead to contemplating the destruction of these states and, beyond them, of the societies concerned. This strategy is currently at work in Iraq, Syria, and elsewhere. The *raison d'être* of the strategy for military control of the world by the triad led by Washington is located entirely in this "realist" vision, which is in direct counterpoint to the naive view—à la Negri—of a globalized state in the process of formation.

(iii) Does the emergence of the globalized production system offer better chances of "catching up" to the countries of the periphery?

The ideological propaganda of the dominant powers—expressed by the World Bank, for example—is devoted to making us believe that if you join in globalization, play the game of competition, you will record respectable, even fabulous, growth rates and improve your chances of catching up. In the countries of the South, social and political forces that support neoliberalism obviously latch on to this discourse. The naive left—again in the manner of Negri—does so as well.

To repeat: if the prospect of catching up by capitalist methods and within globalized capitalism were truly possible, no social, political, or ideological force would be able to block that road, even in the name of another, preferable future for all of humanity. But that is simply not possible: the development of globalized capitalism at all stages of its history, today within the framework of the emergence of a globalized production system just as much as at earlier stages, can only produce, reproduce, and deepen the center/periphery contrast. The capitalist path is an impasse for 80 percent of humanity. The periphery remains, consequently, the "zone of storms." What other option is there, then? There is no other alternative than choosing to construct an autonomous national system based on the establishment of self-sustaining industry combined with the renewal of agriculture organized around food sovereignty. It is not a question of nostalgia for a return to the past—Soviet or national-popular—but the creation of conditions making possible the development of a second wave of awakening for the peoples of the South who could then link their struggles with those of the North who are also victims of a savage capitalism in crisis and for which the emergence of a globalized production system offers nothing. Then humanity could finally advance on the long road to communism, a higher stage of human civilization.

## REFERENCES

About Russia, the Soviet Union, and the Ukrainian conflict, see:

Amin, Samir, *Beyond U.S. Hegemony? Assessing the Prospects* (London: Zed Press, 2006).

———. *Global History: A View from the South.* (Oxford: Pambazuka Press, 2011).

———. "The Return of Fascism in Contemporary Capitalism," *Monthly Review*, vol. 66, no. 4, (September 2014), pp. 1–12.

———. "Russia and the Ukrainian Crisis," *Pambazuka News*, no. 674 (April 17, 2014).

Buzgalin, Aleksandr, "The West-Ukraine-Russia: Multidimensionality of Contradictions, Definiteness of a Position," interview, https://www.youtube.com/watch?v=z7uaK9Qic2A.

## NOTE

1.  Paul Kennedy, *The Rise and Fall of the Great Powers,* (New York: Random House, 1987).

# 3. Thirty Years of Critique of the Soviet System (1960–1990)

Except for individuals with a natural disposition to prophesy, nobody can pretend not to have been somewhat taken aback by the sudden and total collapse of the political systems of Eastern Europe and the USSR. Now that the surprise factor is gone, it is useful to look back at the analyses of these systems that were produced over the course of some thirty years. At the risk of sounding pretentious, I may say that since 1960 I have been part of a small current on the left that had broadly foreseen what came to a climax between 1989 and 1991. Of course, the collapse we thought highly likely was not the only possible outcome of the crisis of the Soviet system. I do not believe in any unfailing linear determinism in history. The contradictions running through every society always find their resolution in diverse responses according to their class content. It was always possible that the Soviet regime might fall to the right (as happened) or evolve (or fall) to the left. The latter possibility has been ruled out for the immediate future but remains on the agenda of history, not only because there is never an end to history but also because I doubt that the right-wing solution in the making will stabilize the societies of the East, even in the medium term.

In rereading what I have written on these topics from 1960 to 1990, I shall not fail to point out the weaknesses and errors brought out by later evolution.

The analyses, judgments, and even forecasts must be put into a context, although they were always more or less affected by the circumstances of the changes under consideration. During these thirty years, the Soviet system has evolved, sought to respond to the crisis, and gone through various phases.

The period following Stalin's death in 1953, and especially from the Twentieth Congress in 1956 to the fall of Khrushchev in 1964, was marked by a first attempt to recover from Stalinism and by the open ideological and political dispute between Moscow and Beijing. The next period of so-called Brezhnev glaciation (immobilist strategy) lasted until the arrival of Gorbachev in 1985. Gorbachev's attempt at perestroika after 1985 ended within a few years in the collapse from 1989 to 1991.

China was at the same time also seeking alternative responses to the problem of building socialism in its own terminology. There was the Maoist attempt from 1961 to 1976, culminating in the Cultural Revolution from 1966 and the gradual slide which led to Deng Xiaoping's economic and political strategy that was characteristic of the 1980s.

The evolutions and successive phases had to be articulated on those operating at a world level. This meant capitalist expansion and the building of the European Economic Community

(EEC) and competition between the United States, Japan, and Europe. It meant military balances between the two superpowers and political responses in the arms race. In the Brezhnev period, it meant Soviet initiatives toward the Third World and conflict with China on the one hand, and U.S. Cold War strategies, including Star Wars preparations after 1980, on the other. Internal options and international policies were intertwined during these thirty years.

Of course, the Soviet system does not date from 1960, and our reflections are based on our analysis of both the 1917 Russian Revolution and the Chinese Revolution, Leninism, Maoism, and Stalinism. It is not our intention to propose a new reading of the seventy-five years of Soviet history. The forty-year period from 1917 to 1957, when successive phases of the evolution of the Soviet system were linked to various moments of world history, will not be examined here, nor will postwar Stalinism and the early Cold War.

I must add a personal note. As an Egyptian, I lived through the Nasserist experience, and from 1960 on I saw that Nasserism would lead to what developed openly from 1971 as Sadat's *infitah* open door: the return to the cradle of compradorization. I felt the same anxieties in the first wave of other "socialist" experiences in Africa—in Algeria, Mali, Guinea, and Ghana—in the first half of the 1960s. The judgment that was at the time rejected by the great majority of the Egyptian and the international left led me to follow the Communist Party of China's criticism of the Soviet leadership. The criticism was made in veiled terms from 1957 to 1958, then openly in the "Letter in Twenty-Five Points" in 1964, and most visibly in the Cultural Revolution after 1966. It was the beginning of a correct response to the "crisis of socialism" before this became a popular theme in the West in 1968.

After 1960, certainly, and even after 1957, I ceased to consider Soviet society as socialist or that the power of the workers was "deformed by bureaucracy," in the famous Trotskyist expression. I had from the beginning regarded the ruling exploiting class (and I do mean *class*) as a bourgeoisie. This class, the *nomenklatura,* saw itself in the mirror of West it aspired to replicate. This is what Mao had perfectly expressed when he was addressing cadres of the Chinese Communist Party in 1963: "You [meaning the Chinese party cadres like those of the USSR] have constructed a bourgeoisie. Do not forget: the bourgeoisie does not want socialism, it wants capitalism."

I drew the logical conclusions from this analysis of the Party and the attitude of the masses toward the authorities. To me it was obvious that the masses did not recognize themselves in the authorities, although they continued to proclaim themselves socialist, but they saw them, rather, as their true social adversaries—and rightly so. In these circumstances, the Party was a long-moldering corpse that had become an instrument of social control over the masses exercised by the exploiting ruling class. The Communist Party, crowning the work of the repressive institutions such as the KGB, organized a network of clients among the people, through control and distribution of all social benefits, even the slightest, thus paralyzing their potential revolt. This kind of party in no way differs from the many one-party systems in the Third World that play the same role (such as Nasserism, the Algerian FLN, the Ba'ath, and the long train of parties in office in Mali, Guinea, Ghana, Tanzania, and others, all who fall under the label of radical nationalism, or in countries, such as the Ivory Coast, who openly opt for capitalism). It is a general pattern suitable for situations where the emergent bourgeoisie has not yet established its ideological hegemony ("the ideology of the ruling class is the dominant ideology in society," said Marx about mature capitalism) and does not appear to exercise legitimate power (this would require a consensus established by the society's adherence to the ideology of its ruling class).

This kind of exercise of power, which fragments the masses through clientship, has a depoliticizing effect, the harm of which should not be underestimated. Events have now shown that in the USSR the depoliticization was of such breadth that the masses believe that the regime they are rid of was socialist, and they ingenuously accept that capitalism is better.

All the elements of the system collapsed like a house of cards as soon as the leaders lost state power. Nobody was prepared to risk their lives to defend an apparatus of this kind. That is why struggles at the top in this kind of party always take the form of palace revolutions, with the grassroots unfailingly accepting those who become winners. I was not surprised by the instant conversion of Nasser's socialist union to Sadatism, nor by the spontaneous disappearances of other parties of the same flavor in many Third World countries. I was no more surprised by the passiveness displayed by "millions" of Soviet communists after 1989.

Even if it was clear to me that Soviet society was not socialist, it always seemed to me to be much more difficult to describe it in positive terms.

I shall not repeat the reasons that made me refuse to believe that fundamental principles of socialism were being implemented, as I have explained them many times. For me, socialism means more than the abolition of private property (a negative characteristic); it has a positive meaning of alternative labor relations other than those defining wage status and alternative social relations allowing society as a whole (and not an apparatus functioning on its behalf) to control its social future. This in turn means a democracy far more advanced than the best bourgeois democracy. In none of these ways was Soviet society different from industrial bourgeois society, and when it moved away from its original goals, it was worse, as its autocratic practice brought it closer to the prevailing model in the areas of peripheral capitalism.

I refused to describe the USSR as capitalist, although its ruling class was in my view bourgeois. My argument was that capitalism means the dispersal of the property of capital as the basis of competition and that state centralization of this property commands a different logic of accumulation. At the political level, I argue that the 1917 revolution was not a bourgeois revolution because of the character of the social forces that were its authors and because of the ideology and social project of its leading forces. This is no average consideration.

I do not attach much significance to a positive description of the system. I have used various terms such as "state capitalism" and "state monopoly capitalism," whose ambiguities I criticized, and finished up with the neutral term "Soviet mode of production." What seemed more important to me was the question of the origins, formation, and evolution of the system and, within this framework, its future.

I was not one of those who always regretted the 1917 revolution. ("It did not have to happen, because the objective conditions for the building of socialism did not exist; it was necessary to stop at the bourgeois revolution.") In my view, the worldwide expansion of capitalism is polarizing, and it is inevitable that the people who are its victims—on the periphery of the system—should revolt against its consequences. One can only support the people in their revolt. To stop at the bourgeois revolution is to betray those peoples, since the necessarily peripheral capitalism that would follow does not provide acceptable responses to the problems that motivated the revolt.

The Russian and Chinese revolutions opened a long transition, the outcome of which is unknown. The dynamic of their evolution may lead to central or peripheral capitalism, and both within the society and on a world scale it may encourage progress toward socialism. What is important is to analyze the objective direction of the advance toward socialism. Along with a minority of the communist left, I continue to support the two theses that seemed to me important in analyzing Soviet evolution.

Collectivization as implemented by Stalin after 1930 broke the worker-peasant alliance of 1917 and, by reinforcing the state's autocratic apparatus, opened the way to the formation of a "new class": the Soviet state bourgeoisie.

Because of some of its own historical limitations, Leninism had unwittingly prepared the groundwork for this fatal choice. I mean that Leninism had not broken radically with the economism of the Second International (of the Western labor movement, it must be said): its concept of the social neutrality of technology is evidence of this.

A society embarking on a long transition faces contradictory demands. On the one hand, it must catch up, in the plain and simple sense of developing the productive forces. On the other hand, in its tendency toward socialism a society in transition offers the alternative of building a society free of economic alienation. The latter characteristically sacrifices the two sources of wealth: the human being reduced to labor power and nature regarded as the inexhaustible object of human exploitation. Can it be done? I always thought the answer was yes, but with great difficulty: a pragmatic compromise to move gradually in the promising direction of the alternative. The economism of Leninism contained the seed of a choice that would gradually make the goal of catching up triumph over the goal of the alternative.

My early adherence to Maoism and to the Cultural Revolution, which I do not repudiate, stems from this analysis. (I was astonished that Lenin had been surprised by Kautsky's betrayal in 1914.) I supported the thesis that Mao established a genuine return to a Marxism that had been distorted by the Western labor movement (and imperialism has its share of responsibility in this drift) even before it was distorted, as it still is, partly, by Leninism.

Maoism offered a critique of Stalinism from the left, while Khrushchev made one from the right. Khrushchev was saying that insufficient concessions have been made to the economic constraints in the technological and scientific revolution, globalization, and the political implications of giving more authority to the enterprise directors, namely the Soviet bourgeoisie. Khrushchev was saying that in these circumstances we would catch up more quickly. Mao was saying that at every step the final goal must be remembered. This was the real meaning of "putting politics in command" (a meaning that has nothing to do with the facile accusation of voluntarism). To avoid losing sight of the final goal, Maoism insisted on equality between workers and peasants (essential in China, but equally so in the Russia of 1930) in order to strengthen their alliance. I explained the goal in terms of what law of value to implement: (i) to surrender to that governing worldwide capitalism and accept thereby peripheral capitalist development; (ii) to envisage building an autocentric national economy, delinked from the world system but analogous to that of advanced capital (the law of value governing the

Soviet statist mode of production and creating a Soviet national bourgeoisie); or (iii) to establish relations between the masses based on the law of value of the socialist transition.

Mao rightly believed, as later evolution in the USSR and China showed, that the question should be handled at the level of power: challenge the monopoly of the Communist Party, crucible of the new bourgeoisie. Hence the big-character poster launching the Cultural Revolution: "Bombard the Headquarters" (of the Communist Party). Was he wrong to believe that it was the only way to increase workers' control over society and to drive the bureaucracy into retreat? He did not believe that concessions to market laws—more power to directors of enterprises, more competition among enterprises—would advance the people's social power. Was he wrong? I am not saying that concessions should not be made to the market. The New Economic Policy had done this successfully in its time. It had to be done, and more bravely than it was, but there were other conditions.

Concessions had to be accompanied by political democratization. The genuine powers of the workers had to be strengthened in this democracy against those of the bourgeois technocrats. The market had to be incorporated into a state policy strongly based on the law of value of the transition to socialism.

The Yugoslavs tried badly and too timidly: too great an opening was made to the exterior; the concessions were too great, worsening internal tendencies to inequality between the republics in the name of competitiveness; and excessive decentralization left the self-managed collectives in a situation of mutual competition. In the USSR, nothing had been done in this direction, or in China, except in the good intentions of the Maoist period, which was later abandoned.

I still believe that Mao was right, even if the later evolution in China seems to contradict this. The evolution does not contradict it but confirms it: concessions to capitalism strengthen the bourgeoisie and weaken the chances of the masses. It is doubtless acceptable and necessary, even today with hindsight, to open the debate on the historical limitations of Mao as has been done for Lenin (his insufficient break with economism) and even for Marx (his underestimation of the polarization inherent in worldwide capitalist expansion).

The central issue concerning the Soviet mode of production was whether it was an unstable solution, characteristic of a transitional period that was evolving toward capitalism or socialism, or a new and stable mode that, despite its faults, indicated the future of other normal capitalist societies.

I offer a self-criticism on this point. I thought at one time, from 1975 to 1985, that the Soviet mode was a stable and advanced form of what the normal tendency of capital should engender elsewhere, by the very act of centralization of capital, leading from private monopoly to state monopoly. There were signs of this at the time. I am not referring to the apparent stability of Brezhnev's USSR. I am referring rather to the earlier theoreticians (Bukharin's theory on state monopoly capitalism) or to propositions of the time: the convergence of systems that Jan Tinbergen detected, bringing together not only the USSR and the advanced West, but also the positions taken by the left-wing social democracies (in Sweden, for example, with the plan for trade unions to buy up industry) and Eurocommunism. It seemed that statist centralization of capital, by suppressing competition and the opacity of the market, produced similarity in the prices charged by the monopolies and those charged by Gosplan. This parallel evolution inaugurated a return to the dominance of ideology.

This ideology was not a return to the metaphysical religions of the tributary age, but the ideology of triumphant commoditization. There was the strong image of George Orwell's *1984* (to whose revived reputation I contributed at the time) and the analysis of the monolithic consensus in the supposedly liberal and democratic societies of the West in Herbert Marcuse's *One-Dimensional Man* that reminded me of my reading of Karl Polanyi. Why couldn't the statist mode be the highest form of capitalism? The Soviet mode foretold a grim future, despite its primitive shape. (How happy Stalin would have been to have the CNN rather than the newspaper *Pravda* to mold a monolithic public opinion, as was done during the Gulf War!)

I added the observation that in the bourgeois revolution the struggle of the peasants against the feudalists did not end in the victory of the oppressed but in the rise of a third party: the bourgeoisie. Why should the battle of the workers (or wage earners) against the capitalists not become the business of the "new class"?

Events proved me wrong. The Soviet regime proved to be unstable, and the offensive of the worldwide right from 1980 was in the opposite direction: deregulation and privatization had their heyday.

I return to my self-criticism with a subtle distinction. Never mind that the Soviet model was incapable of becoming a definite alternative to be gradually copied by others. Events have shown that it was not. This may reflect only its own weaknesses. It does not mean that in other parts of the developed world, once the recent wave of liberal utopia is over, evolution may not follow a path mapped out by the old USSR.

I have returned to considerations more remote from the present and the instability of the transition in which the Soviet model indicates a historic cycle now complete. It seemed to me that the description "socialist phase" was more deceptive than useful. I accept that this might be described as primitive socialism. Even before the breakup of the Soviet system in 1989, it seemed to me that it was more fruitful to describe the transition as "national and popular." This stressed the contradiction between the goals of this phase and the logic of worldwide capitalist expansion (a contradiction symbolized by the description as national, in reference to my concept of delinking). It stressed the contradictory content of the popular bloc, which was neither bourgeois nor proletarian with a socialist vocation. The long transition is by nature unstable. It may lead to capitalism, as happened in the USSR. It may lead somewhere else, and I shall return to this in the conclusion.

An assessment is needed of the Soviet cycle now that it is completed. It is not positive overall, or negative. The USSR, and subsequently China and even the countries of Eastern Europe, has built modern autocentric economies such as no country of peripheral capitalism has succeeded in doing. According to my analysis, this is because the Soviet bourgeoisie was produced by a popular, national, and so-called socialist revolution, whereas the bourgeoisies of the Third World, established in the wake of the worldwide expansion of capitalism, are generally of a comprador nature. The ambiguous character of the socialist aspect of the revolution has shaped a society in which the workers have won social rights (the right to work and to social welfare) that have no match even in developed, central capitalist societies (where some of the rights were belatedly won by great struggle, usually after the world wars, in part because of the fear of communism), never mind in peripheral capitalist societies.

Today the overt capitalist option of the USSR and Eastern Europe returns to the agenda the peripheralization of their economy and society for which the popular classes (and even the local bourgeoisie) are unprepared because of the depoliticization wrought by blind statist despotism. I had underestimated the depoliticization and the disastrous effects that have now become evident, and I thought that the peoples and ruling classes of the East would be able to control the evolution toward capitalism to which the latter aspired through reforms associated with the gradual passage to political democratization. I thought that in these circumstances the popular classes might bend the evolution toward the general advance of socialism. The socialist aspirations of workers for social rights and a more active role in the management of their workplace and country would be more evenly balanced with the demands of the market, including but not restricted to the aspirations of the bourgeoisie. A revived national popular alliance would reopen debate on socialism on a world scale in the West and on the periphery. I must offer some self-criticism on this point, as this prospect is now ruled out and the rightist evolution toward crude capitalism is irreversible. I may not be wrong in the long term, however, when the results of this peripheralization become evident, when the workers realize that the drastic fall in their standard of living is not a momentary sacrifice imposed by the transition.

The Soviet system long ago entered the phase of acute crisis, which has become terminal. The system failed repeatedly to go from the successful extensive accumulation of the first half of its existence to intensive accumulation. The failure showed that what existed in the Soviet Union was not a capitalist mode of production, as that by definition is based on intensive accumulation. I analyzed the crisis in terms of social struggles through the resistance of workers, thanks to the right to work and because enterprise directors do not have the

legitimacy of a boss in the West. I said that an end had come to
the social compromise characteristic of the first phase of the
system, which allowed extensive accumulation (and underlying this, a degree of popular modernization in mass education,
broad social mobility, and so on). Palmiro Togliatti, followed
by Enrico Berlinguer, said this too. It was necessary either to
go further with the leftist critique of Stalinism or to accelerate
rightist evolution toward a normal capitalism or elitist modernization of a Third World kind. The bourgeoisie chose the
latter: the market, the old story of putting the masses to work
through the threat of unemployment, and privatization, to
stabilize the bourgeoisie by restricting social mobility, which
had emerged as a demand in the later years of the system.

I have always refused to treat the specific crisis in the Soviet
mode alongside the totally different crises of capitalism. I have
also rejected those analyses of the system offered by the capitalist propaganda machinery and vulgarized in the media.

The distinction between an economy of poverty—socialism—and an economy of abundance—capitalism—leads to
an empty ideological discourse. It is obvious that the poverty
shown in long lines, for example, was produced by the voluntary freezing of prices, which permitted broad access to
consumer goods, which was a concession to egalitarian pres-
sures from the masses and the middle strata. It is obvious that
if prices rise massively, there are no more lines, but the seem-
ingly vanished poverty is still there for those who no longer
have access to consumer goods. The shops in Mexico and
Egypt are packed with goods, and there are no lines in front of
the butchers' shops, but meat consumption per head is a third
of what it was in Eastern Europe. This childish argument has
made a fortune for the Hungarian J. Kornai, who is promoted
by the World Bank.

The command economy, as compared to the self-regulating economy made fashionable by U.S. academics, is also an outrageous simplification. The real Soviet economy was always based on a mixture of adjustments by the market operating outside the plan and administrative orders, especially on investment. The market idealized by the prevailing liberal ideology has never been self-regulating beyond the constraints of the social system where it operates and the state policies that determine its framework. The real problem is that accumulation in the framework of statist centralization of capital (corresponding to an integrated state-class) differs from capitalist accumulation, which in the modern age results not from market laws defined in an ideal abstract but from competition among monopolies.

From as early as 1935, the priority of the economic apparatus shifted to military expenditure. Does this mean that the Soviet system is military? It is suggested by some that it has a natural expansionism through conquest. Similarly, Jean Jaurès posited that "capitalism bears war within itself like the cloud the storm." This is ideological nonsense. Analysis of the relative significance, and social burden, of military expenditure cannot be conducted purely on the grounds of modes of production. Military expenditure should be analyzed from the structure and conjuncture of national or local and international or regional global systems. From this viewpoint, it is obvious that the arms race was imposed on the USSR by its real enemies and false friends among the capitalist powers.

The discourse on "totalitarianism" lacks coherence. It has pretentious academic forms in the style of Hannah Arendt or childish forms in the media. A U.S. president used the phrase "Evil Empire" to describe the U.S.'s adversary and came close to the kind of language used by Iran's Ayatollah Khomeini.

Was it forgotten that a society grown amorphous would never be able to rid itself of despotism?

I saw in Sovietism an attempt to escape the impasse of Stalinism by going to the right rather than the left. The proposals illustrated what I called "the utopia of constructing a capitalism without capitalists." The Novosibirsk School, which most influenced Gorbachev, pushed the logic of Léon Walras to the limit. It imagined a pure and perfect self-regulating market. As Walras had understood, and Enrico Barone had been explaining since 1908, this did not call for dispersed private property but for total statist centralization of property. Proponents of the Novosibirsk School called for the constant bidding for access to means of production by all individuals who were free to sell their labor or organize production as entrepreneurs. The old dream of Saint-Simon, the scientific management of society taken up by German social democracy (Engels was the first to see it as the dream of capitalism without capitalists), expresses the economistic alienation of all bourgeois ideology, whose unreal and utopian character was shown by historical materialism.

This philosophy is the key to the reformist vision of Khrushchev and Gorbachev and even the adulterated version of the Brezhnev period. History has shown that these concepts were untenable and that the drift to the right would reach its goal in the transformation of the Soviet bourgeoisie into a normal, private property–owning bourgeoisie.

The revolution of the years from 1989 to 1991 was top-down from the ruling class and not bottom-up from the people. The same was true of Sadat's counterrevolution in 1971; it was not a counterrevolution but the speeding up of a tendency that was latent in Nasser's period. The Western media would like to present the revolutions in the East as blows for freedom;

they neglect to analyze the vulnerability of democratization, which may very well be only a means of ensuring a transition to crude capitalism, a system that is always despotic, as can be seen from the historical experience of the capitalist peripheries. I disagree. The revolutions can be considered blows for freedom only if the system was overtaken by the left. In their present form, these movements were no more than prodigious and unexpected accelerations of the natural evolution of the system, despite the thesis of totalitarian blockage.

Gorbachev thought he could control the reform process and did not expect to be dumped by the majority of the *nomenklatura* class he represented (as Boris Yeltsin's rise showed), any more than he expected the irrelevance of the Communist Party, which proved to be useless for transmitting the project to the popular level. The Soviet *nomenklatura* bourgeoisie will be the bourgeoisie of tomorrow, directly appropriating the means of production into private hands and no longer collectively through the intermediary of the state. This is not a social revolution but a political upheaval so vast that it requires radical change among the leadership. (This was also the case in Sadat's counterrevolution.) The parallel rise of a stratum of new rich adventurers (the "mafia" in the USSR) is similar to the so-called parasitic bourgeoisie in Egypt. It was difficult to avoid the sudden political fragmentation of the former *nomenklatura* and the manipulation of the national aspirations of the peoples of the former Soviet Union. This is, of course, the business of the Western powers. They will easily take advantage of the situation through the blackmail of financial aid. They will push the frontiers of Russia back to those of sixteenth-century Muscovy and demolish any hope for the country to be a significant competitor on the world scene.

Here too I offer a self-criticism. I thought—like Gorbachev—that the system was capable of reform and that on this occasion—even though the reform plan was rightist in its vision of economic management—the promising democratic element would enable the popular forces to bend the evolution to the left. I underestimated the disastrous impact of depoliticization, which made the working classes vulnerable and unable to make beneficial use of democratization and devise a positive counterplan. Their disarray left them passive and deluded, easy prey for nationalism. The depoliticization was no less dramatic for the ruling class, and it was tamed by the supreme authority. The ruling class was fragmented into conservatives, Gorbachev supporters, right-wing populists, and so on, and the top-down reform became impossible. I thought the big power nationalism of this class would be a safeguard. I underestimated the ferocious appetite of the candidates for consumerism, as they were ready to sacrifice all for the speedy satisfaction of their desire to be rich. I also overestimated the Soviet patriotism of the popular classes, who could not have cared less about satisfying the real needs of their country. The rejection of patriotism may be healthy in some respects; in the long term it permits the social project to be brought to the foreground. The rejection of patriotism is also exceedingly dangerous in the short term, as external adversaries will not fail to exploit it in order to peripheralize Russia and the other nations of the former Soviet Union and turn them into Europe's—especially Germany's—own Latin America.

For the USSR, as for any other historical society, the external political options were closely linked to the demands of the internal social dynamic. I was never convinced by the ideological thesis that the USSR was intrinsically aggressive or was always peace loving. I suggested, rather, a realistic analysis of the way the internal and external dynamics could operate in the USSR, in China, and in the various regions of developed capitalism (United States, Japan, and Europe). I considered various scenarios for the world system and degrees of probability. In this context, the correct or distorted projection of reality by the ruling classes cannot be ignored. This is true of all authorities in office, Soviet or other.

Obviously there is no guarantee of the correctness of a realistic analysis. Any analysis is influenced by passing events and may be extrapolated in a way that is subsequently disproved. I shall give some examples that provide a motive for self-criticism.

An analysis of the USSR's external policies and their assessment from a humanist, democratic, and socialist outlook on a world scale must explicitly refer to the world system in which the policies under criticism were implemented.

Until the 1960s, the Soviet system was fairly isolated and on the defensive. The view I took at the time still seems correct—even with hindsight. I put forward several positions that I shall only summarize here.

Not for a moment since 1917 have the fascist and democratic Western powers abandoned the idea of defeating the Soviet Union. Despite the USSR's decisive role in defeating the Axis powers, it emerged exhausted from World War II and was threatened by the United States' nuclear monopoly. The Yalta agreements were not a division of the world between victorious imperialisms but a minimum guarantee the Soviet Union had won for its own security.

The Soviet Union, like China, Vietnam, or Cuba, has never sought to export revolution but has on the contrary always practiced prudent diplomacy, with the primary purpose of defending its own state. All the revolutions were conducted virtually against the will of Big Brother: China against the advice of Moscow, and Vietnam and Cuba acting on their own. This fact never shocked me, and I tried to fathom the reasons, without accepting that revolutionaries must submit to the dictates of the Soviet Union. Revolutionaries should rather go further and be self-reliant. Successful revolutionaries have done this (as seen in China, Vietnam, Cuba, Kampuchea, and Nicaragua).

The Cold War was Washington's initiative after 1947. The USSR stuck rigidly to the division at Yalta (hence its attitude to the revolution in Greece), and never in its history did it nurture a project to invade Western Europe. Talk of Soviet bellicosity is pure Western propaganda. The Zhdanov doctrine of a world divided into two camps was characteristically defensive (justifying the nonintervention of the USSR beyond the Yalta boundaries) and inaugurated a period of Western isolation of the USSR, and of China, after 1949. The Atlantic powers never once ceased interfering in the Third World with colonial wars, Israeli aggression, and so on.

The USSR and China began to leave their isolation after the 1955 Bandung Conference, when they saw the advantage they could gain from giving support, albeit limited, to Third World liberation movements.

The belated Soviet military effort after 1970 contributed to a genuine balance of deterrence. Then, but only then, did the USSR become a superpower and a new era began.

The bipolarity of the twenty years before the Soviet collapse of 1989–1991 is asymmetrical in that the USSR was a superpower only in military terms and was not able to compete with the Western imperialists in their capacity for economic intervention.

There was never any symmetry between the actions of the two superpowers and their impact. The United States, with Europe and Japan in the background, pursued a diplomacy of clear goals and familiar methods to ensure domination of the periphery (access to raw materials, markets, military bases, and so on). The United States established hegemony through this shared strategy, and when U.S. economic advantage over its allies began to erode, it used this strategy to maintain its declining hegemony (the Gulf War is the most recent episode).

The goals of Soviet intervention beyond the Yalta boundaries are more difficult to identify. I have argued that the main goal was to breach the Atlantic alliance by separating Europe from the United States. The Soviets achieved this mainly through support of Third World liberation movements and national radical governments (Palestine and the Arab world, the Horn of Africa, Angola, Mozambique, and the "African socialist" states). Europe was reminded of its vulnerability and dependence on oil supplies and encouraged to distance itself from the United States and to negotiate. The strategic aim was not to weaken Europe and invade but to bring it to active, peaceful coexistence capable of supporting the USSR's economic development, a development moving to the right. De Gaulle was the only European political leader to understand—and accept—this approach. The Soviet scheme failed, and neither Khrushchev's carrot nor Brezhnev's stick produced the desired result any more than the renewed carrot from Gorbachev and Yeltsin persuaded the Europeans to abandon their own agenda of weakening the USSR as much as possible and to encourage its breakup.

Soviet support of Third World peoples and governments was naturally limited. I have always been sympathetic to this without ever underwriting its theoretical legitimations, such as the "noncapitalist road," which I have criticized on occasion as damaging to the success of Third World progressive forces. I was, of course, vilified by the sycophants of the Moscow Academy, including some who now head the roll of anticommunists, and by the unconditional supporters of the USSR in Africa, the Middle East, Cuba, and Vietnam.

I did not see Soviet interventions as an aggressive determination to export revolution and to dominate, but rather as a defensive posture from comparative weakness despite the acquisition of parity in nuclear deterrence.

The interventions have sometimes been perceived as a manifestation of growing strength. This requires consideration of the debate on "social imperialism," a term devised by the Chinese in 1963. It was a plan for a social compromise between the Soviet bourgeoisie and its people, a revisionist compromise. It was, after all, similar to the social democratic compromise in the West and would have allowed external expansion similar to the colonial expansion supported by the imperialist consensus in the West. There was nothing startling or unimaginable in the concept. The real issue was not whether the Soviet bourgeoisie did or did not want to embark on it but whether it was capable of it. I think the answer to this remains open.

There were clear signs that at least some Soviet authorities dreamed of following this path. In the 1960s, a plan of aggression against China was initiated with the overt goal of dismembering China and dividing it between the USSR, Japan, and the Western powers. Moscow backed off a few years later.

Brezhnev's regime continued to look strong from the outside and was so judged in most anti-socialist analyses of the time. I had my own reservations on this apparent strength and found in this the explanation for Brezhnev's abandonment of an aggressive attitude to China. I voiced the fear that the regime might trip up, as the useless invasion of Afghanistan hinted, and was relying increasingly on military strength rather than persuading the world of its socialist beliefs. It made concessions that suggested economic difficulties and the relatively limited success of the rightist line it adopted to overcome them.

I have pointed to the limitations and risks of various analyses from 1970 to 1990 of the possible scenarios for the evolution of the world system. Such analysis has its merits, as it demands an explanation of what is too often left unexplained in analyses not carried to a logical conclusion. I shall pass by the various debates in which I participated. Some of the debates are finished. There is no mileage now in the notion of strengthening Soviet social imperialism on a world scale by taking advantage of U.S. decline and bringing together the Soviet's revisionist compromise with a Europe of the left. That may never have been more than a joke. I did take it seriously for a while. I made the mistake of underestimating the internal weaknesses of the Soviet system and overestimating the European left.

The debate about a broad realignment of international alliances, a Paris–Bonn–Moscow axis and a Washington–Tokyo–Beijing axis, is ongoing. The realignment could lead to a European Atlantic role, a wider gap between the United States and Europe, or a European shift to the left. The arguments remain valid, although the probability of a particular scenario rises or falls. I raised four issues that remain central even now after the collapse of the Soviet system.

Can the integration of the East in the world system be a significant element in the outcome of the crisis of world capitalism now that "socialism" no longer exists? The question raised more than five years ago is even more pertinent now, although the answer I gave seems to me to have been contradicted by events in the short term. I said then that the bourgeois Soviet Union would control its integration into world capitalism.

Is it feasible to reconstitute an integrated world market? This question too dates back more than five years and remains current. This is regardless of whether the Soviet Union, when integrated into the market, would occupy its place as a new capitalist center or as a new industrialized periphery. I maintain my principled stand that the idea of reconstituting the integrated world market is utopian.

Are state and nation active subjects of history in the way that class is? This question arises from the weakening of serious social struggles in the modern world, which is to the immediate benefit of states engaged in conflict or rivalry or those emerging from the disintegration of multinational states. This is the familiar debate that dates from the 1960s and is based on the Chinese theory of three worlds: "states seek independence, nations liberation, and peoples revolution." I shall say no more except that I do not find what I wrote at the time to have been contradicted by current events—indeed, much the reverse. My thesis on chaos picks up this discussion and carries it into the circumstances of our time.

Are changes leading toward a Eurasian bloc of Europe and the USSR, in de Gaulle's terms, or toward Gorbachev's plan for a "common house"? Has this nightmare prospect for the United States been avoided by Europe's vacillating policies and internal contradictions, the Atlantic alliance, and the coming together of Moscow and Washington? I believe the immediate result has provided a second wind for U.S. hegemony, eclipsing Europe again to the benefit of the United States' shining seconds, Japan and Germany.

The collapse of the Soviet system, although it has been predictable for a long time, is a major event of our time. All scenarios for the future must take the new circumstances into account.

Does the collapse mean an end to socialism and Marxism or, as the major media like to say, the "end of history," the triumph of a monolithic consensus ensuring the perpetual survival of the capitalist ethos? I believe this is nonsense, even though an era is obviously ending.

The era of Socialism I established in the nineteenth century, ended in 1914 with the failure of the social democratic parties of the Second International, which became overt accomplices in their national imperialisms. Lenin was right to declare Socialism I dead at that moment.

Its successor, Socialism II, of the Third International and Leninism, is now dead after a long illness. Since 1963, I have been writing that the advance of socialism required a rupture with Sovietism as radical as that made by Lenin in 1914. It is also significant that the Soviet system, in its overt recruitment to capitalism, takes the same position that prevails in Western culture against the Third World, namely against three-quarters of humankind.

The death of a child does not bring the parent back to life. The grandchild must carry on the task of the ancestors. Long live Socialism III, to come.

Are the outlines of this Socialism-to-come already visible?

I believe they are, and I have the temerity to put forward the three lessons I have learned in the past thirty years in my dual critique of the Soviet system and capitalist globalization:

(i)   Creating an alternative must come before catching up, at all costs.

(ii) World polarization implies that delinking is the only choice, even if the means must constantly be reviewed in light of the constraints of general evolution.

(iii) Systematic action must be undertaken to rebuild a polycentric world, thus providing scope for the people's autonomous progress.

These three conditions determine a potential and necessary renaissance for an internationalism of all the people on Earth to combat the internationalism of capital. It offers a prospect, albeit distant one, of a socialism that can only be worldwide and able to meet the challenge of globalization. Otherwise it will rapidly decline and perish.

A decade ago I suggested opening a debate on the transition beyond capitalism. I took a long look at history, free of the scholastic distinction between reform and revolution, and I suggested that there were two forms of transition. One I described as revolutionary, although possible through a range of consistent reforms; it entailed a certain ideological consciousness capable of expressing the demands of a new social project. This was the passage to capitalism. The other implied no ideological consciousness. The objective constraints determined events. This one was decadent, since it implied the anarchic breakup of the old system. An example was the passage to European feudalism.

The tributary centralization of the Roman Empire became an obstacle to the advance of the barbarian peoples. Advancement demanded fragmentation of the centralization represented by feudalism. A new centralization of surplus has now been achieved by capitalism. In the same way, today's centralization of surplus by capitalism on a world scale has become an obstacle to the advance of three-quarters of humankind. The rebuilding of a unified world system, a system beyond capitalist polarization, requires, therefore, a breakup of the system of capitalist centralization of surplus. It requires delinking.

Will humankind be able to control this transition to some degree? It can do so only through the renaissance of a serious worldwide movement of Socialism III. In the alternative, the objective constraints will allow the long decadence of society, through redoubled violence of senseless conflicts or barbarism. In an age such as ours—when there are enough weapons to destroy the whole Earth, when the media can tame the crowds with frightening efficiency, when short-term egoism or anti-humanist individualism is a fundamental value threatening Earth's ecological survival—barbarism may be fatal.

More than ever, the choice we face is not capitalism or socialism, but socialism or barbarism.

# 4. Lenin and Stalin: Facing the Challenge of the Century

*Communist Revolutionaries Faced with the Challenges of Reality*

L
enin, Bukharin, Stalin, and Trotsky in Russia and Mao, Zhou Enlai, and Deng Xiaoping in China shaped the history of the two great revolutions of the twentieth century. This chapter examines the experiences of Russia and China, with no intention of dismissing other twentieth century socialist revolutions (North Korea, Vietnam, Cuba).

As leaders of revolutionary communist parties and then later as leaders of states, they were confronted with the problems of a triumphant revolution in countries of peripheral capitalism and forced to "revise" (a term considered sacrilegious by many) the theses inherited from the historical Marxism of the Second International. Lenin and Bukharin went much further than Hobson and Hilferding in their analyses of monopoly capitalism and imperialism and drew this major political conclusion: the imperialist war of 1914–1918 (they were among the few, if not the only ones, to anticipate it) made necessary and possible a revolution led by the proletariat. Bukharin wrote *Imperialism and the World Economy* in 1915 and Lenin wrote *Imperialism, the Highest Stage of Capitalism* in 1916.

With the benefit of hindsight, the limitations of their analyses can be highlighted here. Lenin and Bukharin considered imperialism to be a new stage in the history of capitalism ("the highest") connected with the development of monopoly capitalism. To challenge this thesis, historical capitalism has always been imperialist, in the sense that it has led to a polarization between centers and peripheries since its origin (the sixteenth century), which has only increased over the course of its later globalized deployment. The nineteenth century pre-monopolist system was no less imperialist. Great Britain maintained its hegemony precisely because of its colonial domination of India. Lenin and Bukharin thought that the revolution, which had started in Russia ("the weak link"), would continue in the centers (Germany, in particular). Their hope was based on an underestimation of the effects of imperialist polarization, which inhibited revolutionary prospects in the centers.

Nevertheless, Lenin, and even more so Bukharin, quickly learned the necessary historical lesson. The revolution, made in the name of socialism (and communism), was, in fact, something else: it was mainly a peasant revolution. So what was to be done? How can the peasantry be involved with the construction of socialism? By making concessions to the market and by respecting newly acquired peasant property? By progressing slowly toward socialism? The New Economic Policy (NEP) saw the implementation of this strategy.

Yes, but Lenin, Bukharin, and Stalin also understood that the imperialist powers would never accept the Revolution or even the NEP. Soviet Russia, even though it was far from being able to construct socialism, was able to free itself from the straitjacket that imperialism always wants to impose on all peripheries of the world system that it dominates. In effect, Soviet Russia delinked from the imperialism of the West. After the hot wars of intervention, the Cold War was to become permanent, from 1920 to 1990. The imperialist West, like the Nazis, could not even tolerate the very existence of the Soviet Union. For their part, Lenin and Stalin attempted to make the West understand that they did not intend to export their revolution. They sought peaceful coexistence by all the diplomatic means at their disposal. Between the two world wars, Stalin had desperately sought an alliance with the Western democracies against Nazism. The Western powers did not respond to this invitation. On the contrary, they sought to push Hitler's Germany to make war on the Soviet Union. The unfortunate Munich Agreement of 1937 and the rejection of Stalin's appeals in 1939 attest to that. Stalin fortunately defeated the strategy of the "democratic" powers by making a last-minute agreement with Germany following the invasion of Poland. Later, with the entry of the United States into the war, Stalin renewed his attempts to found a lasting postwar alliance with Washington and London. He never gave that up. But again, the policy of peaceful coexistence sought by the Soviet Union was defeated by the unilateral decision of Washington and London to end the wartime alliance by initiating the Cold War following the Potsdam Agreement, when the United States had a monopoly over nuclear weapons. The United States and their subaltern NATO allies systematically pursued a relentless "roll back" policy from 1946 to 1990 and beyond. NATO, presented to the unsuspecting as a defensive alliance against the aggressive ambitions attributed to Moscow, has revealed its true nature as an aggressive organization with the annexation of

Eastern Europe and the new missions taken on in the Middle East, the Mediterranean, the Caucasus, Central Asia, and now in Ukraine.

What was the Soviet leadership to do? Attempting to push for peaceful coexistence by making concessions, if necessary, and refraining from intervening too actively on the international stage was one option. Yet at the same time, it was necessary to be armed to face new attacks, which were difficult to avoid. That implied rapid industrialization, which, in turn, came into conflict with the interests of the peasantry and thus threatened to break the worker-peasant alliance, the foundation of the revolutionary state.

SINCE 1947, THE UNITED STATES OF AMERICA, THE dominant imperialist power of that epoch, proclaimed the division of the world into two spheres, that of the "free world" and that of "communist totalitarianism." The reality of the Third World was flagrantly ignored: one was privileged to belong to the "free world," as it was "non-communist." "Freedom" was considered as applying only to capital, with complete disregard for the realities of colonial and semi-colonial oppression. The following year Zhdanov, in his famous report (in fact, Stalin's), which led to the setting up of the Cominform (an attenuated form of the Third International), also divided the world into two: the socialist sphere (the USSR and Eastern Europe) and the capitalist one (the rest of the world). The report ignored the contradictions within the capitalist sphere, which put the imperialist centers in opposition to the peoples and nations of the peripheries who were engaged in struggles for their liberation.

The Zhdanov doctrine pursued one main aim: to impose a peaceful coexistence with the United States and their subaltern

European and Japanese allies, hence calming their aggressive passions. In exchange, the Soviet Union would accept a low profile, abstaining from interfering in colonial matters that the imperialist powers considered their internal affairs. The liberation movements, including the Chinese Revolution, were not supported with any enthusiasm at that time, and these carried on by themselves. But their victory (particularly that of China, of course) was to bring about some changes in international power relationships. Moscow did not perceive this until after Bandung, which enabled the Soviet Union, through its support to the countries in conflict with imperialism, to break out of its isolation and become a major actor in world affairs. In a way, it is not wrong to say that the main change in the world system was the result of this first awakening of the South. Without this knowledge, the later affirmation of the new "emerging" powers cannot be understood.

The Zhdanov report was accepted without reservation by the European and Latin American communist parties of that era. However, almost immediately, the report came up against resistance from the communist parties of Asia and the Middle East. This was concealed in the language of that period, for the Asian and Middle Eastern parties continued to affirm "the unity of the socialist camp" behind the USSR, but as time went on, resistance became more overt with the development of their struggles for regaining independence, particularly after the victory of the Chinese Revolution in 1949. Few, if any, have ever written the history of the formulation of the alternative theory, which gave full rein to the independent initiatives of the countries of Asia and Africa, which would later crystallize at Bandung in 1955 and then in the constitution of the Non-Aligned Movement (which from 1960 was defined as Asian-African, plus Cuba). The details are buried in the archives of some communist parties (those of China, India, Indonesia, Egypt, Iraq, Iran, and perhaps a few others).

Nevertheless, I can bear personal witness to what happened, having been lucky enough, since 1950, to participate in one of the groups of reflection that brought together the Egyptian, Iraqi, and Iranian communists, and some others. Information about the Chinese debate, inspired by Zhou Enlai, was not made known to us until much later, in 1963. We heard echoes of the Indian debate and the split that it had provoked, which was confirmed afterwards by the constitution of the Communist Party of India (CPM). We knew that debates within the Indonesian and Filipino communist parties developed along the same lines.

This history should be written as it will help people to understand that Bandung did not originate in the heads of the nationalist leaders (Nehru and Sukarno particularly, rather less, Nasser) as is implied by contemporary writers. Bandung was the product of a radical left-wing critique that was at that time conducted within the communist parties. The common conclusion of these groups of reflection could be summed up in one sentence: the fight against imperialism brings together, at the world level, the social and political forces whose victories are decisive in opening the way to possible socialist advances in the contemporary world.

This conclusion, however, left open a crucial question: Who will direct these anti-imperialist battles? Would it be the bourgeoisie (then called "national"), whom the communists should then support, or a front of popular classes, directed by the communists and not the bourgeoisie (who were anti-national, in fact)? The answer to this question often changed and was sometimes confused. In 1945, the communist parties concerned were aligned, based on the conclusion formulated by Stalin that the bourgeoisie everywhere in the world (in Europe, aligned with the United States, as in the colonial and semi-colonial countries, in the language of that era) have "thrown the national flag into the rubbish bin" (Stalin's phrase) and the communists were therefore the only ones who could assemble a united front of the forces that refused to submit to the imperialist, capitalist American order. The same conclusion was reached by Mao in 1942, but only made known (to us) when his *New Democracy* had been translated into Western languages in 1952. This thesis held that for the majority of the peoples of the planet the long road to socialism could only be opened by a "national, popular, democratic, anti-feudal and anti-imperialist revolution, run by the communists." The underlying message was that other socialist advances were not on the agenda elsewhere, that is, in the imperialist centers. Such revolutions could not possibly take shape until after the peoples of the peripheries had inflicted substantial damage on imperialism.

The triumph of the Chinese Revolution confirmed this conclusion. The communist parties of Southeast Asia, in Thailand, Malaysia, and the Philippines in particular, started liberation struggles inspired by the Vietnamese model. Later, in 1964, Che Guevara held similar views when he called for "one, two, three Vietnams."

The avant-garde proposals for initiatives by the independent and anti-imperialist countries of Asia and Africa, which were formulated by the different communist groups of reflection, were precise and advanced. They are to be found in the Bandung program and that of the Non-Aligned Movement. The proposals focused on the essential need to reconquer control over the accumulation process (development that is auto-centered and delinked from the world economy).

It so happens that some of these proposals were adopted, although with considerable dilutions made by the governing classes in certain countries, in both Asia and Africa, between 1955 and 1960. At the same time, the revolutionary struggles waged by all the communist parties of Southeast Asia were defeated (except in Vietnam, of course). The conclusion would seem to be that the "national bourgeoisie" had not exhausted its capacity for anti-imperialist struggle. The Soviet Union also came to that conclusion when it decided to support the non-aligned front, while the imperialist triad declared open warfare against it.

The communists in the countries concerned were then divided between the two tendencies and became involved in painful conflicts that were often confused. Some drew the lesson that it was necessary to support the powers in place that were battling imperialism, although this support should remain critical. Moscow gave wind to their sails by inventing the thesis of the "non-capitalist way." Others conserved the essentials of the Maoist thesis, according to which only a front composed of the popular classes that was independent of the bourgeoisie could lead a successful struggle against imperialism. The conflict between the Chinese Communist Party and the Soviet Union, which was apparent as early as 1957 but officially declared in 1960, of course confirmed the second tendency among the Asian and African communists.

However, the potential of the Bandung movement wore out within some fifteen years, emphasizing—if it should be needed—the limits of the anti-imperialist programs of the national bourgeoisie. Thus the conditions were ripe for the imperialist counter-offensive, the re-compradorization of the Southern economies, if not—for the most vulnerable—their recolonization. Nevertheless, as if to give the lie to this return imposed by the notion of the definitive and absolute impotence of the national bourgeoisie—Bandung having been, according to this vision, just a "passing episode" in the Cold War context—certain countries of the South have been able to impose themselves as "emerging" in the new globalization dominated by imperialism. But emerging in what way? Emerging markets open to the expansion of capital of the oligopolies belonging to the imperialist triad? Or emerging nations capable of imposing a genuine revision of the terms of globalization and reducing the power exercised by the oligopolies, while reconducting the accumulation to their own national development? The question of the social content of the powers in place in the emerging countries (and in the other countries of the periphery) and the prospects that this opens up or closes is once again on the agenda. It is a debate that cannot be avoided: What will—or could—be the "post-crisis" world?

Would the results be better now, when a second awakening of the South is on the horizon? Above all, will it be possible this time to build convergences between the struggles in the North and in the South? These were lamentably lacking in the Bandung epoch. The peoples of the imperialist centers then finally aligned behind their imperialist leaders. The social-democrat project of the time would in fact have been difficult to imagine without the imperialist rent that benefited the opulent societies of the North. Bandung and the Non-Aligned Movement were thus seen as just an episode in the Cold War, perhaps even manipulated by Moscow. In the North, there was little understanding of the real dimensions of this first emancipatory wave of the countries of Asia and Africa, which, however, was convincing enough for Moscow to give it support.

The period in question was not really the "bipolar world" of the Cold War, but a multipolar world (the West, the Soviet East, China, and the South) that forced imperialism to retreat.

LENIN, BUKHARIN, AND STALIN'S EQUIVOCATIONS are understandable, then, because they were faced with the challenges presented by the agrarian question and the aggressiveness of the Western powers. In theoretical terms, there were U-turns from one extreme to the other. Sometimes a determinist attitude inspired by the phased approach inherited from earlier Marxism (first the bourgeois democratic revolution, then the socialist one) predominated; sometimes it was a voluntarist approach (political action would allow a leap-over stage). Finally, from 1930 to 1933, Stalin chose rapid industrialization and armament (and this choice was not without some connection to the rise of fascism). Collectivization was the price of that choice. Here again, we should refrain from making too hasty conclusions: all socialists of the time (and even more so, the capitalists) shared Kautsky's analyses on this point and were convinced that the future belonged to large-scale agriculture. The idea that the modernized family farm is more efficient than large-scale farms would have to wait a long time before being accepted. Agronomists (particularly those of the French school) understood before economists that the extreme division of labor in the industrial model was not suitable in agriculture. The farmer is faced with the requirements of a variety of tasks that are difficult to predict.

The break in the worker-peasant alliance implied by the choice of collectivization was the origin of the abandonment of revolutionary democracy and the autocratic turn.

Would Trotsky have done better? In my opinion, he would certainly not have. His attitude toward the revolt of the Kronstadt sailors and his later equivocations demonstrate that he was no different than the other Bolshevik leaders in government. But, after 1927, living in exile and no longer having responsibility for managing the Soviet state, he could delight in endlessly repeating the sacred principles of socialism. He became like many academic Marxists who have the luxury of asserting their attachment to principles without the need to be concerned about being effective in transforming reality. There are pleasant exceptions among Marxist intellectuals who, without having had responsibilities in the leadership of revolutionary parties, let alone revolutionary states, have nonetheless remained attentive to the challenges confronted by state socialisms (such as Baran, Sweezy, Hobsbawm, and others).

The Chinese communists appeared later on the revolutionary stage. As a result, Mao was able to learn from Bolshevik equivocations. China was confronted with the same problems as Soviet Russia: revolution in a backward country, the necessity of including the peasantry in revolutionary transformation, and the hostility of the imperialist powers. But Mao saw more clearly than Lenin, Bukharin, and Stalin. Yes, the Chinese Revolution was anti-imperialist and anti-feudal. But it was not bourgeois democratic; it was popular democratic. The difference is important: a popular democratic revolution necessitates maintaining the worker-peasant alliance in the long run. That allowed China to avoid the fatal error of forced collectivization and instead made all agricultural land state property, gave the peasantry equal access to use of this land, and renovated family farms. Thus, Mao gave a new response to the agrarian question based on renovated small family farms, without concomitant small property ownership, thereby reducing migration toward the cities and making it possible to combine the strategic objective of food sovereignty with the construction of a complete and modern national industrial system. This system is certainly the only possible response to the agrarian question for all countries in the contemporary South, even if the political conditions allowing its implementation have only come together in China and Vietnam.

The two revolutions had difficulty in achieving stability because they were forced to reconcile support for a socialist outlook and concessions to capitalism. Which of these two tendencies would prevail? These revolutions only achieved stability after their "Thermidor," to use Trotsky's term. But when was the Thermidor in Russia? Was it in 1930, as Trotsky said? Or did it occur with the NEP in the 1920s? Or was it during the ice age of the Brezhnev period? And in China did Mao choose Thermidor beginning in 1950? Or do we have to wait until Deng Xiaoping to speak of the Thermidor in 1980?

It is not by chance that reference is made to lessons of the French Revolution. The three great revolutions of modern times (French, Russian, and Chinese) are great precisely because they looked forward beyond the immediate requirements of the moment. With the rise of the "Mountain" led by Robespierre in the National Convention, the French Revolution was consolidated as both popular and bourgeois and, just like the Russian and Chinese Revolutions, which strove to go all the way to communism even if it were not on the agenda due to the need to avoid defeat, retained the prospect of going much further later. Thermidor is not the Restoration. The latter occurred in France, not with Napoleon, but only beginning in 1815. Still it should be remembered that the Restoration could not completely do away with the gigantic social transformation caused by the Revolution. In Russia, the restoration occurred even later in its revolutionary history, with Gorbachev and Yeltsin. It should be noted that this restoration remains fragile, as can be seen in the challenges Putin must still confront. In China, there has not been (or not yet) a restoration. Florence Gauthier, and a few other historians of the French Revolution, do not assimilate Thermidor to restoration, as the Trotskyist simplification suggests.

## REFERENCES

Roberts, Geoffrey, *Stalin's Wars: From World War to Cold War, 1939–1953*, (New Haven, CT: Yale University Press, 2008).

Kautsky, Karl, *The Agrarian Question*, (London: Pluto Press 1988).

Amin, Samir, "China 2013," *Monthly Review*, New York, vol. 64. no. 10, (March 2013), pp. 14–33.

Hobsbawm, Eric, *Echoes of the Marseillaise: Two Centuries Look Back on the French Revolution*, (London: Verso Books, 1990).

# 5. Out of the Tunnel?

Previous chapters portrayed the place that the Eurasian space (with borders from Poland to China) occupied in the successive stages of the formation of the global system and, in this context, explained how Eurasia defined the challenges faced by the Russian Empire and subsequently the USSR. This chapter focuses on the challenges that post-Soviet Russia has faced since that time. However great the transformations that have taken place in Russia over the course of the last fifteen years may appear, they are not "revolutionary" (or "counter-revolutionary")—they are the result of the acceleration of underlying trends that were already in existence within the Soviet system in the 1930s, and they have been gathering force since then.

I will not limit myself on this subject to stating that Soviet society at the time of the USSR's dissolution was no longer "socialist," as the promoters of the 1917 revolution wanted, but rather it was a specific type of capitalist society (which I described as "capitalism without capitalists"), destined to become "normal" capitalist society (i.e. capitalism with capitalists). This is indeed the plan of the new ruling class (which sprang from the preceding ruling class, no less) even though, as we shall see, the reality of this system falls extremely short of this plan.

## Basic Characteristics of the Late Soviet System

The Soviet system can be defined by five basic characteristics: corporatism, autocratic power, social stabilization, economic delinking from the global capitalist system, and integration into the global capitalist system as a superpower. The concept of "totalitarian regime," popularized by the dominant ideological discourse, is shown here as elsewhere to be flat and hollow and incapable of taking account of Soviet reality, that is, how the system was managed and the contradictions that led to the evolution and transformation under way.

### 1. CORPORATISM

The Soviet system was a corporatist regime, which refers to the fact that the working class (supposed to become "ruling" class) had lost its unifying political consciousness both through the purpose of the policies put in place by those in power and through the objective conditions of the rapid mushrooming of their numbers during accelerated industrialization. The workers of each enterprise, or group of enterprises, forming a "combinat," together with their management and directors constituted a social/economic "block" and defended their place within the system. These "blocks" confronted each other on all levels: in negotiations between ministries and departments of Gosplan and in daily dealings with enterprises from combinats other than their own. The unions, reduced to work management (monitoring work and employment conditions) and managing the social benefits of workers, found their natural place in this corporatist system.

The corporatism in question had a crucial role to play in the reproduction and expansion of the system as a whole. It involved a double substitution of (i) the principle of "profitability" that, in the last resort, governs decisions to invest in capitalism and (ii) the market that, in capitalism, still defines the way in which prices are determined. Corporatism constituted the reality that "planning" hid through its intentions to gain acceptance for a so-called scientific rationale of the macro-economic management of the production system.

Corporatism emphasized the regionalist dimension in the negotiations between competing blocks. This regionalism was not based on the principle of "national" diversity (as in Tito's Federal Yugoslavia). The relationship between Russia—the dominant nation both numerically and historically—and other nations was not a colonial one. The redistribution of investment and social benefits that operated to the detriment of the Russians and to the benefit of the peripheral regions is evidence of this. In this regard, comparing the USSR to an "imperial" system dominating its "internal colonies" in spite of the impression of the "dominance" of the Russian nation (and even the arrogance of some of its expressions) is nonsense. Perhaps the Baltic states will learn that they have exchanged an advantageous position from which they benefited as part of the USSR for a subjugated position within the European Union! The Caucasians and the peoples of central Asia will be brutally dealt with as colonies by the Westerners, having lost the bargaining power that they enjoyed within the USSR.

The regionalism in question concerned small regions (within the republics to which they belonged) with common interests to defend in a global system that ensured their inter-dependence, which was in fact always more unequal than Gosplan's rationalizing discourse claimed.

## 2. AUTOCRATIC POWER

The choice of this term is not intended to weaken the cri-tique of the system; "the absence of democracy" is easy to see whether representative (elections here bore no surprises) or participative, as imagined by the revolutionaries of 1917. The unions and all possible forms of social organizations had been compelled to submit to central state control, effectively prohibiting participation in decision making on all levels.

But this fact provides no explanation of the pseudo-concept of "totalitarianism." Autocratic power was disputed within the ruling class, the representatives of the corporate blocks. What to outward appearances was an autocracy masked the reality of a power that rested on the "peaceful" resolution of corporatist conflicts through consideration for one another.

Here again, the autocratic management of the conflicts in question necessarily took on regional dimensions. The struc-ture of the system comprised a pyramid of powers ranging from the management (always autocratic) of local interests to those of the union and the republics. This regional dimension, sometimes but not necessarily "ethnic," facilitated the breakup of the union and the threatened breakup of the republics (Russia first), which is today a dangerous challenge for central powers.

## 3. SOCIAL STABILIZATION

The extreme violence that accompanied the building of the Soviet system cannot be ignored. These violent acts varied.

The major conflict pitted the defenders of the socialist plan at the origin of the revolution against "realists" who, in practice if not in their rhetoric, gave absolute priority to "catching up" through accelerated industrialization/modernization. This conflict was the inevitable result of the objective contradiction that the revolution faced. It was necessary to "catch up" (or at least reduce the gap) as the revolution inherited a "backward" country (the expression "peripheral capitalism" here is preferable), and simultaneously build "something else" (socialism). This contradiction is at the heart of the problems related with overcoming capitalism on a world scale (that is, the "long transition from capitalism to global socialism"), but this won't be discussed here. The victims of this first major cause that led those in power to resort to violence were communist militants.

A second type of violence accompanied accelerated industrialization. Some aspects of this type of violence can be compared to the violence that accompanied the construction of capitalism in the West, the massive migration from the countryside to the towns and the wretched circumstances associated with proletarianization (overcrowded accommodation, and so on). The fact remains that the USSR carried out this construction in record time—a few decades—compared with the entire century it took in central capitalist countries. The latter benefited from the extra advantages of their dominant imperialist positions and the option of allowing their "surplus" population to emigrate to the Americas. The violence of primitive accumulation in the USSR is, in this respect, no more tragic than it was elsewhere. On the contrary, no doubt, for the accelerated industrialization in the USSR allowed the children of the popular classes to benefit from massive social mobility unknown in the countries of central capitalism dominated by the bourgeoisie. In spite of everything else, it is this "specificity" inherited from original socialist intentions that won the majority of the working classes and even "collectivized" peasantry over to the system, even if it was autocratic.

Furthermore, let us not forget the violence committed by the dominant global capitalist system: military intervention, the most savage Nazi aggression, and economic blockades.

The Soviet system, however contradictory it may have been, succeeded in building a social order capable of stability and was in fact stable during the post-Stalin period. Social peace was "bought" by moderation in the exercise of power (although still autocratic), the improvement of material conditions, and the tolerance of "illegal" discrepancies.

Certainly, stability of this kind is not destined to last eternally, but no system is, in spite of the claims made by ideological discourse (be it "socialist" or capitalist "liberalist"). Soviet stability masked the contradictions and limitations of the system, which summed up its difficulty in passing from extensive forms of accumulation to intensive forms of the latter, just as it had difficulty emerging from autocracy and allowing the democratization of its political management. Yet this contradiction might have found a solution in an evolution toward the "center left," which includes the opening-up of market spaces (without challenging the dominant forms of collective property) and democratization. Perhaps this was the intention of Gorbachev, whose failed attempt—naïve in many ways—brought down the regime "on the right" from 1990 onwards.

## 4. ECONOMIC DELINKING FROM THE GLOBAL CAPITALIST SYSTEM

For the most part, the Soviet production system was effectively delinked from the dominant global capitalist system. The rationale that governed the economic decisions of those in power (investments and pricing) did not derive from demands for "open" integration into globalization. It is thanks to this disconnection that the system succeeded in progressing as swiftly as it did.

This system was not, however, wholly independent of the rest of the capitalist world. No system can be, and the delinking, as defined here, is not a synonym of autocracy. Through its integration in the global system, the USSR occupied a peripheral position, mainly as an exporter of raw materials.

## 5. INTEGRATION AS A SUPERPOWER

Through the success, rather than the failure, of its construction, the USSR worked its way up to the rank of military superpower. It was the Soviet army that defeated the Nazis and then succeeded, in record time, in ending the United States' nuclear and ballistic monopoly. These successes are at the origin of the USSR's political presence on the postwar world scene. In addition, Soviet power benefited from the prestige of its victory over Nazism and that of "socialism," which it claimed to be the expression of, whatever the illusions concerning the reality of this "socialism" were (it was sometimes described as "really existing socialism"). The USSR made "moderate" use of it in this sense, contrary to the affirmations of anti-Soviet propaganda, and the Soviets did not set out to "export the revolution" or to "conquer" Western Europe (this was the spurious motive used by Washington and the European bourgeoisie to get NATO accepted). The USSR did, however, use its political (and military) might to compel dominant imperialism to pull back from the Third World, opening up a margin of autonomy for the dominant classes (and the peoples) of Asia and Africa, which they lost with the fall of the USSR. It is not by chance that the United States' hegemonic military offensive developed with the violence we have witnessed from 1990 onwards. Soviet presence from 1945 to 1990 imposed a multipolar organization on the world.

## New Forms of Capitalism in Russia

I use the terms of the title of this section deliberately, thus avoiding the term "neoliberalism." This expression, which I use like everyone else because it is imposed by dominant discourse, should in fact rule out any serious thinking, for it only concerns (dubious) ideological rhetoric.

Neoliberalism, or more generally, liberalism, will be called into question both in the West and in the East when its failure is recognized. In fact "liberalism" is to "really existing capitalism" what "socialist" discourse was to "really existing socialism": an ideological tool designed to eliminate the analysis of true questions. Liberalism promises everything at once: effectiveness (without defining the terms), democracy, peace, and even social justice. The implementation of the policies practiced in its name produces almost the opposite, in fact: stagnation (and in some cases even decline), the deterioration of democracy (or even the reinforcement of autocracies), permanent war, and increasing inequality. Yet it matters little, and we are asked to wait.

The collapse of the Soviet system, reinforced by the populism of the Third World and the erosion of the social-democratic commitment in the West, has allowed so-called liberal ideology to triumph and led to vast support for its discourse. This is true in Russia as elsewhere. Incidentally, as Germany and Japan had "lost the war but won peace," Russia would, thanks to liberalism, undertake accelerated and (finally) effective modernization in democracy. We forget—or pretend to forget—that Washington's objective is not to allow the rebirth of a strong Russia (any more than that of a strong China), even if it were capitalist, but to destroy it.

Have fifteen years of "reforms" culminated in the establishment of a Russian capitalist system capable of stabilizing the country and effectively putting it on the path of liberalist promises? Reality obliges us to answer no: the USSR has disintegrated and in turn Russia lives under the threat of disintegration, and none of the institutions in place (its private enterprises or its state) are equipped to carry out the necessary investments to improve the effectiveness of the production system (on the contrary, disinvestment is massive). The systematic destruction of the Soviet system's positive achievements (education in particular) does not point to a brighter future. It is difficult to see how a system with these characteristics could stabilize without understanding its stabilization, for a time, at such a level of complete destitution and powerlessness.

So, in fact, these new forms of capitalism in Russia have increased rather than reduced the characteristics of a Soviet system that has reached an extreme stage of decline.

1. THE INTEGRATION OF THE NEW RUSSIA AS
A MINOR PERIPHERY OF THE CONTEMPORARY
IMPERIALIST CAPITALIST SYSTEM

"Open" Russia is not only an exporter of raw materials (oil first and foremost); it is liable to become no more than that. Russia's industrial and agricultural production systems no longer benefit from the attention of the authorities and are of no interest to the national private sector or to foreign capital.

There has been no investment worthy of the name to make industrial and agricultural progress possible and these systems only survive at the expense of the continued deterioration of Russia's infrastructure. The capacity for technological renewal and the high-quality education that underpinned it in the Soviet system is being systematically destroyed.

Who is responsible for these massive declines?

First, of course, is the new ruling class, which for the most part originated from the former Soviet ruling class and who was made fabulously rich, no doubt, through the privatization/pillage from which it has benefited. The concentration of this new class has, moreover, reached such uncommon proportions that the term "oligarchy" suits them perfectly. The similarity with the oligarchies of Latin America is certainly striking. This class owes its increasing wealth to three sources: income from oil (which depends on world circumstances such as the high or low prices of crude), the cannibalization of industries (privatized industrial firms are not destined to form the basis of increased and more efficient production but only to allow the oligarchies to survive through their decline), and commissions from opening the country's markets up to imports. Rent income and commissions still define a comprador bourgeoisie, not a "national" bourgeoisie.

Imperialism benefits from and supports the country's decline to the rank of minor periphery. Essentially, as far as Russia and other former USSR republics are concerned, the United States plans to reduce them to the rank of minor de-industrialized and therefore powerless peripheries. In other words, their aim is to "Latin-Americanize" the former Soviet East (the former USSR and Eastern Europe). The methods are designed in varying proportions depending on the case, ranging from total destruction for countries with a revolutionary past (Russia and Yugoslavia) to a milder form of subordination in "conservative" Eastern Europe (Poland, Hungary).

Of course, in the context of this common vision shared by the powers-that-be in the United States and in Europe, a certain competition may be revealed between the different associates of the imperialist triad. Who will have the most to gain from this Latin Americanization, the United States or Western Europe? The current compromise leaves eastern Europe mainly to Germany and Russia to the United States. NATO (under the preponderant influence of the United States), the WTO, and Brussels (whose liberal options only serve to strengthen those of the WTO) are entrusted with the task of "managing" this essentially asymmetrical system. The fact remains that the management of the political responsibilities of collective imperialism is riddled with contradictions, which are beyond the scope of this chapter. European/American competitiveness is at work in the context of this management, and in this respect Washington has several cards to play that cannot be ignored. These include, obviously, London's unwavering Atlanticist option and also that of the servile political classes of eastern Europe. Europe missed the opportunity to build a rapprochement with Russia that would have, for sure, reinforced its autonomy vis-à-vis the U.S. hegemonic attitude.

The oligarchy's explosion of wealth has led to the formation of a new middle class known as the "new" Russians. The jobs these people hold are entirely unproductive and derived from the oligarchs' spending, whereas the former middle class, made up of professionals and engineers who were in general far more highly qualified and certainly more productive, have ended up with the popular classes and among the victims of this comprador capitalist development. Moreover, the monopolistic oligarchies, the exclusive beneficiaries of state generosity, make the formation of a class of authentic and inventive entrepreneurs impossible. They are persecuted by mafias and the state itself, making the appearance of capitalism "from the base" impossible.

The liberal discourse, according to which the winners of the system are the most highly qualified and inventive individuals while the losers are the "least productive" workers, does not stand up to any serious examination. In actual fact, the losers are all those working in production in the new Russia.

2. IRRESPONSIBLE AUTOCRATIC POWER:
THE CAPITALIST FORMS OF THE NEW RUSSIA
EXCLUDE ALL DEMOCRATIC PROGRESS.

Autocracy is no longer a "vestige of the past" here but a necessary form of the comprador oligarchy's power. The new constitution of 1993 serves this power, and the constitution's creation established a presidential regime that reduced the powers of the Duma (elected parliament) to nothing. As we know, Western governments pretend to ignore the 1993 constitution, saving their reproaches for the democratic deficit in the only regimes that resist liberalism while they approve the dictatorship of those that serve it.

The distinguishing feature of the new autocracy, as compared with the former one, lies elsewhere. Namely, the difference lies in the totally irresponsible character of the power that it exerts. The autocracy is at the service of the oligarchy and takes part in the battles that the clans are engaged in even though it knows how to ensure it is paid for services rendered. In fact, this autocracy has placed itself at the service of globalized oligopolistic foreign capital, which it implements without the slightest resistance from the *diktats* issued by the WTO, the IMF, and even NATO.

The conflicts that recently pitted Putin against certain oligarchs have not brought about significant change in the organization of the system. Putin's objectives remain limited: first of all, he aims to strengthen the positions of the clan of the St Petersburg oligarchs (the new president's client base) to the detriment of the others; then—perhaps—to "rationalize" the system by separating more distinctly autocratic presidential state bureaucracy from the class that it has never renounced serving. Each has his role, but all are part of the same play.

Are the Russian people responsible for this decline? Certainly, to some extent, although this responsibility is mitigated somewhat by the utter confusion they find themselves in following the brutal collapse of the Soviet institutions (sometimes destroyed by cannon fire, as was the case with the first elected parliament). The new political parties had no social or ideological basis that would have allowed them to emerge from their inexistence. The new "right," reduced, in fact, to individual irresponsible cliques originating from the former system, has certainly successfully handled demagogic rhetoric amplified by the corrupt media that is at their service. Their stories are no less rapidly used, as they are faced with a generally intelligent public opinion that is evidence of the considerable politicization of the Russian people. Because of this, the new right rapidly found itself a prisoner of the support of the bureaucratic power of the new autocracy. The fact remains that the Communist Party, in spite of the hopes placed in it by a large minority of the electorate (nearly 50 percent), did not know how to reinvent itself (and move away from its legacy of the autocratic administration of power) or even resist the pressure of the new dictatorship. On the contrary, the Communist Party has facilitated its establishment by subscribing to the new constitution. The Party then tried to make people forget its stupid cowardice and the major errors that it made by initiating an ambiguous "nationalist" discourse. But the embryonic political parties of the alternative left have not proved their capacity to undermine the plans of the new oligarchy and have rapidly withdrawn into intellectual chapels isolated from the popular classes.

## 3. DEGENERATED AND WEAKENED CORPORATISM

Faced with the obtuse and declining Communist Party, the trade unions could have provided effective resistance as they have retained the respect and support of their members, who number in their millions, for at least twelve years.

The major error made by trade union leaders was to think that the former corporatism that surrounded them could guarantee their survival. It is true that the objective situation facilitated this error of judgment and perspective. In the great majority of cases, directors and people in managerial positions in the enterprises excluded from the new system of oligarchic powers remained "on the side of their workers" in the daily fight for the survival of production. For their part, some social-democrat ideologists cherished the illusion that the establishment of the tripartite combination that they recommended (employer, union, state) allowed a kind of positive "historical compromise." These ideologists were a war too late—social democracy in the West having already announced its conversion to liberalism—and were not sufficiently aware that the model of peripheral capitalism under construction in Russia excluded all "social" forms of managing it.

The cowardice of trade union management and the illusions that they were under did not prevent social struggles from breaking out here and there, nor did it prevent power from being pushed back, as was the case with the resistance of the railway workers, which threatened to bring the country to a halt. However, these struggles did not succeed in bringing about much-needed reviews in the methods of trade union management, and the attempts of a few groups from the new left to reestablish working-class life on independent and new union bases achieved no more than anecdotal success.

This combination of unfavorable factors sowed the seeds of the decline of the trade union organizationa, which has been seen over recent years. The collapse of the social services that the trade unions had managed under the Soviet system has contributed to this disaffection.

## 4. UNCONTROLLED REGIONALISM

The strong regionalism of aging Sovietism has entered a phase of destructive decline. Regionalism was formerly controlled, and not necessarily through state violence, by the responsible concern of the Soviet autocracy to accept the necessary compromises.

The clans of the new irresponsible autocracy think, on the contrary, that it is useful to exploit regionalism to serve their short-term objectives. In some cases this adverse trend has gone very far, and this is borne out by the Chechen situation.

That there were serious questions waiting to be answered in certain regions, especially in the "non Russian" areas of the Russian Federation, cannot be ignored. No one can doubt that external forces tried to exploit these difficulties, including, of course, the United States and their Islamic allies in the case of

Chechnya. However, Moscow is responsible for the deterioration of the situation. A large majority of the Chechen people rejected the "Islamists'" appeals for secession. Those in power in Russia refused the support of this majority and deliberately opted to play the military intervention card with scant regard for the consequences of this decision. Clearly this was the product of mediocre calculations on the part of the clans of the oligarchy (who were interested, for example, in the route of the oil line from the Caspian Sea) and the state bureaucracy (who wanted to rebuild "the unity of the Russian people" and obtain their "unconditional" support in the face of "the external and terrorist enemy").

It is known that the terrorist attacks in Moscow and elsewhere, which have not been proven to be the work of Chechens, have fulfilled similar functions to September 11, which was exploited by the Bush administration.

In this respect too, Putin's administration does not seem to have broken with the errors made by Yeltsin. The second Chechen war undertaken by Putin resulted in the same failure as the first and has been exploited in the same way as by the two preceding presidents. Putin can be credited with a reform of the territorial organization of the powers designed to put an end to regionalist flare-ups. The fact remains that this reform is still commanded by the principle of the autocracy (doubling an elected governor by a kind of appointed prefect) and refuses to rely on the populations concerned (which would risk strengthening their capacity for resistance to the pressure exerted by the oligarchs). The reform undertaken is therefore not likely to favor the correct solution of open or latent conflicts.

### 5. RUSSIA REMOVED FROM THE INTERNATIONAL SCENE

Since Putin came to power, Russia has held a minor position in the G7, now G8 (G71/2). Yet for all that it is not an active player in the functioning of global balance. To all appearances, Russia preserves considerable military power: it is second in the world in terms of its nuclear equipment and ballistic missiles, although the deterioration of its military organization gives reason to fear that it may be incapable of using this arsenal effectively in the event it were necessary, which is to say, in the event of United States' aggression.

It goes without saying that this removal poses a problem for the future of the global system. Which camp will Russia join in the event that political differences between certain European countries (France and Germany) and the United States succeed in splitting Atlanticism, which is still in command of the collective imperialism of the triad, or if the conflict with certain southern countries (China, or even India, Iran, or North Korea) were to grow? Certainly in the short term, the question does not arise: Europe remains Atlanticist in spite of the gnashing of teeth by a certain few. Even if Russia were to align itself, like China, with France and Germany in order to not give Washington *carte blanche* in Iraq, the gesture has not brought about a switch of alliances. Moscow is still hitched up to the American cart in spite of some (moderate) defiance. Washington made no mistakes in that respect and reserved its violent condemnation for the French alone. The pressure exerted by the military presence of the United States in central Asia and the Caucasus, their recent establishment in Georgia, and their manipulation of the Islamic threats have so far managed to keep Russia out of the big international game. Russia could derail the U.S.

plan aimed at reducing Russia's economy to the status of a
minor subordinated periphery by playing an active role in
the revival of a "southern front," including China. But Russia
did not choose this way, but rather the opposite. Russian calculations are based on the illusion that only its alliance with
the United States can protect it from eventual Chinese expansionist ambitions in Siberia and central Asia. By acting on
these calculations, in fact, Russia reinforces the U.S. plan of
isolating its major potential competitor: China. Russia will
most likely not be paid back for this "service," which will
only accelerate its decline.

Yet the fact remains that all these balances (or imbalances)
that benefit the United States remain fragile, and the certain
failure of the U.S. intervention in Iraq will sooner or later end
up calling it into question.

Will Russian diplomacy find its place with a new dealing of
the cards? I will come back to this question, which is one of
the major dimensions of the construction of an alternative to
liberal American globalization.


## 6. IDEOLOGICAL DECLINE

Soviet ideology continued to feed on supposedly "socialist"
rhetoric. Even severely depleted, Soviet power knew that its
legitimacy lay in the Revolution of 1917. This is irritating and
even derisory. Yet the distance that separated this rhetoric
from Soviet reality was no greater than that which separated
liberal discourse from really existing capitalism, and just as a
good number of normal individuals support liberal discourse
in spite of the social catastrophe that accompanied the reality
of it, it should come as no surprise that socialist discourse has
had its believers up to the very last.

The new oligarchic autocracy needs to take the opposite view of Soviet discourse, but it does not know what to replace it with. Stories about economic effectiveness and democracy are not credible in Russia even though they may be in eastern Europe. "Patriotic" discourse, therefore, constitutes this power's last hope, now that it finally has its back against the wall. The rhetoric in question serves to remove the real problems (social inequality, the destruction of the 1917 conquests, the ineffectiveness of new economic management, and the loss of the international role of the country) while pretending "to unite the whole country behind its leaders," implying that Russia's leaders resist dominant globalized capital.

Note here that this comprador bourgeoisie discourse closely resembles that of other ruling classes with the same type of development in Asia and in Africa. All comprador classes that rule contemporary peripheries try to give themselves a "patriotic" image although they are responsible for the decline that their nations are suffering and in fact only facilitate the (foreign) domination of international capital.

Patriotism, in a positive sense, is (now more than ever) certainly necessary in Russia, as it is elsewhere, and it is faced with the challenges of American liberal globalization. It is important that Russian patriotism be conceived as a positive element in the construction of self-sustaining development, remains open to all working classes, and does not become demagogic and deceitful rhetoric, as is the case with the discourse of the new Russian power.

The fact remains that the ideological discourse of the new Russian power has no real hold over its people. Evidence for this can be seen in its increasing need to resort to elections that are openly falsified on a large scale. In other words, we are dealing with a power devoid of legitimacy and credibility, or perhaps this new Russian capitalism is incapable of finding a center of gravity around which to stabilize its power.

The opposition's deficiency is also revealed by its ideological discourse. Communist Party leaders have rallied round the "patriotic" discourse of power, barely giving it more precise contents. Rather like those in Muslim countries who, "threatened" by the wave of political Islamism, try to surpass their opponents in their chosen field in the belief that in this way they will exorcise the latter's powers of attraction. Others invoke "Euro-Asianism," that is to say, nationalism that is both anti-American and anti-European, and recommend a rapprochement with Asia (China, India, and Iran). This rapprochement would certainly be one of the requirements for the formation of an alternative globalization. However, there is no need for dubious para-ideological legitimacy, which only distances support for modernist universalism, even if it is of "Western" origin and therefore, thus far, is deformed by the reality of the imperialist system of which the West is the center.

There is no doubt that serious alternative views derived from a criticism of Sovietism from the left, who aim to forge ahead with socialist reconstruction, would find favorable terrain in Russia. However, there is no choice but to accept that up till now these visions have not moved out of left intellectual circles and have no hold on the people.

### Is There a Worthwhile Alternative in Russia Today?

The picture of Russia portrayed in the preceding pages may seem seriously pessimistic with regard to the future of the country. In fact, the failure of new Russian capitalism and its inability to provide the conditions for stabilization should, on the contrary, be reason for optimism. It is sometimes said in Moscow that Russia, as on the eve of 1917, is almost ripe for a new revolution or for a radical transformation capable of redressing the direction of evolution. With what local and global perspectives could this occur? Under what conditions?

The basic principles on which the alternative to the current system should be established are simple, clear, and in fact largely understood. Internally ("nationally"), this alternative would be based on (i) a "mixed economy" that on the one hand gives the state the means to orient overall development and on the other offers private property and the market a sufficient profit margin to make the promotion of initiatives possible; (ii) the institutionalization of worker/enterprise/state collective bargaining; and (iii) the development of representative democracy through the promotion of participative democracy initiatives. On a global scale it would incorporate (i) the organization of the negotiation of forms of economic management (trade, capital flows, technological transfers, monetary management) based on the acknowledgment of the diversity of interests and the inequality of the partners; and the (ii) acknowledgment of the sovereignty of the people reinforced by support for the progress of democratization, which are the foundations of a multipolar political world. The implementation of all of these principles would make it possible to begin an initial stage on the road to the "long transition to world socialism."

Of course, these very general principles that are valid for all (China or Russia, Germany or the Congo) only come into their own when put into practice in a way that respects the diversity of objective situations.

For Russia this means the following: (i) the re-nationalization of large enterprises, particularly in oil and energy (therefore expropriating them from the oligarchy); (ii) the invention of new forms of joint management (workers and leaders) of the industrial and commercial enterprises, whether these should be formally public (state, communities, workers collectives) or private; (iii) the reestablishment and reinforcement of public social services, education (which was of a high standard in the USSR), and scientific and technological research; (iv) the abolition of the constitution of 1993 and the elaboration of an authentically democratic constitution by a large elected convention; (v) support for forms of popular intervention of participative democracy; (vi) the initiation of extensive nego-tiation between the republics of the former USSR to enable the construction of an economic and political regional space that respects the autonomy of the partners and is capable of establishing interdependence to the benefit of all; (vii) the re-establishment of Russian military power (until there is a general disarmament, when the United States is prepared to submit to one); (viii) the development of negotiated com-mercial, technological, and financial arrangements initiating the construction of a "great Europe" from the Atlantic to the Pacific; and (ix) the development of a foreign policy that is active, independent (of United States policy in particular), and designed to strengthen the institutions responsible for the con-struction of a multipolar world.

From the perspective of the alternative globalization envis-aged here, the place and the roles fulfilled by the national partners shall by force of circumstance remain specific and dif-ferent from one another. Russia shall occupy the place of both a major producer/exporter of raw materials (oil and mineral products) and a renewed industrial power (without being necessarily subject to the hazards that the search for "competi-tiveness" on a so-called open world market implies). China's place, by comparison, is that of a new industrial power whose production would be commanded principally by the enlargement of its internal market and only accessorily by its exports (the opposite of the principle that the WTO is determined to impose). This option would mean in China, as elsewhere in Asia and Africa, appropriate solutions to the agrarian problem based on acknowledgment of the right of access to land for all peasants. Certainly, Russia also still has an agrarian problem (as does eastern Europe) that cannot be resolved by the development of capitalism as it was in the developed centers of the global system. But the questions are posed here in rather different concrete terms from those that characterize the countries of the "Third World" (Asia, Africa, and Latin America) and require appropriate solutions.

The government of Yevgeny Primakov had well and truly begun a recovery program along the same lines as those described here with, it seems, plenty of determination but also considerable prudence in the first measures taken (which is easy to understand). As Gorbachev might have wished to do but did not know how, Primakov envisaged the construction of a "center left" economic and political system. First, Primakov was the victim of the inability of the Communist Party (still powerful at the time) to understand and support the initiative. He was also the victim of international hostility, mainly from the United States, but, unfortunately, also from Europe, which did not abandon its intention to "Latin-Americanize" the former USSR (and also Eastern Europe through the process of its integration into the European Union).

In this struggle, the responsibility of the people is always primary, in Russia as elsewhere. The intensification of social struggles and democratic demands, the dissipation of illusions, and the beginning of the reconstruction of new and open left forces that are able to convince the working classes that the Communist Party and the unions continue to treat them as "supporters" in the service of their short-term political calculations are all positive signs of a possible Russian recovery.

Europe has no less responsibility than it does now. It could reach out to Russia and abandon its ongoing partnership in the collective imperialism of the triad, which forces it to be part of the hegemonic plans of the United States. For that, it would have to leave behind the "shifting sands" in which it is mired.

Perhaps Putin has now understood that the objective of the United States and its European allies is to destroy Russia and not to help it renew itself. But the system on which his government is based does not allow him to resist the destructive attacks of the imperialist triad effectively. To do that, he would have to give up his support for the oligarchy that exploits and oppresses the Russian people. Otherwise the strategy of the Atlantic powers will be allowed to develop without effective resistance.

The examples of Georgia and Ukraine highlight the situation. Through the support that the Russian government gave to the local autocrats that were considered to be friends, Moscow made heroes out of individuals who are really only vulgar foreign agents!

For thirty years, the United States and Europe have benefited from the contempt with which the governments inherited from Sovietism have treated democracy, and, consequently, they have been and still are sitting pretty. Wałęsa, friend of Washington and the Pope, pretended to be the leader of a movement to "renew the working class" (that is how Solidarność was presented), while his real project was to destroy the capacity of the working class to resist the attacks of capitalism. (When Solidarność came to power, it did not give the factories to the workers, but instead closed them or gave them to foreign capital!) The legitimate democratic aspirations of the peoples of the East are manipulated and led astray all the more easily since the predominant left in Europe is complicit with dominant imperialism. Consequently, that left does not help with the necessary reconstruction of a post-Soviet left, but, on the contrary, contributes to the continuation of the confusion.

The geopolitical shapes of possible alliances among the United States, Europe, and Russia will heavily influence the nature of future globalization. Different forms are possible, two of which are the consolidation of the "Russian-American alliance" based on Russia's choice to become a major petroleum exporter and nothing more, or a special European-Russian partnership. The "common war on terrorism" has come, since September 11, 2001, to consolidate the former alliance, at least in appearance.

Facts amply demonstrate that this completely asymmetrical partnership is nothing more than the implementation of Washington's plan to destroy Russia. Far from supplying Russia with the means to modernize its productive system, this partnership is narrowly tied in with the interests of the Russian oligarchy and its submission to the project of transforming Russia exclusively into a supplier of raw materials. Moreover, this partnership has facilitated the penetration of the United States into the Caucasus and Central Asia, from where Moscow is being ousted. This kind of alliance, then, cannot be an element in building an alternative globalization.

The other possible alliance can be such an element. A quite different European-Russian partnership could be designed if it were not limited to facilitating the export of Russian petroleum to Europe but included the active support of Europe to the modernization of the entire Russian productive system. Europe could have taken the initiative in 1990 and proposed a partnership capable of strengthening the autonomy of the two partners in relation to the United States. Europe, fearful as usual, did not do so, too afraid to go against Washington. Therefore the way was opened for the U.S. offensive against Moscow. Russian petroleum is thus intended primarily to satisfy American needs and is sold in dollars. A partnership that would have allowed for its sale primarily to Europe and in Euros would have considerably reduced European dependence on suppliers largely controlled by Washington, whether in the Middle East, the Caspian, or the Gulf of Guinea. Europe has thus accepted the quite unequal sharing of the spoils from the former Soviet world: the United States gets Russia and Central Asia and the Europeans get Poland and the Baltic states.

Assuming that Europe pursues its Atlanticist orientation, which seems the most probable course of action, Russia has other cards to play. A coming together of the large Eurasian powers—Russia, China, and India—that would involve the rest of the Old World (the Arab world and Africa) is necessary and possible, and it would put a decisive end to Washington's project to extend the Monroe Doctrine to the whole world. Putin's Eurasian project seems to be part of this possibility. This must undoubtedly be done with patience, but above all with determination. Moreover, the chances for the success of this project would be strengthened if there were increased opposition to the power of the oligarchy in Russia.

# 6. The Ukrainian Crisis and the Return of Fascism in Contemporary Capitalism

The preceding chapters place the Soviet Union and contemporary Russia in the world system dominated by the imperialist powers of the triad (United States, Europe, Japan). Not long ago, these powers were in continual conflict, but today they work together in a form of collective imperialism (Amin, 2013). They treat the rest of the world as a field for expanding their control, particularly over access to natural resources, and even their exclusive use, if necessary. Delinking, or even the slightest desire to open up some margin of autonomy in the system, is anathema to them. To fight these aspirations of the people, nations, and states of the periphery, all means are implemented, from military aggression to the services of fascist movements. The Soviet Union was, consequently, an enemy to bring down. The Cold War against the Soviets between 1920 and 1990 and the attempts to use the ambitions of Nazi Germany against "Judeo-Bolshevism" were key elements of this effort. New Russia, despite its capitalist choice, remains a potential enemy insofar as it refuses to accept the colonized peripheral status the powers of the triad want to impose on it. Within this context, the return of the question of fascism, exploited by the collective imperialism of the triad, allows us to better understand the stakes involved in both the current Ukrainian conflict and the "Eurasian" project.

It is not by chance that the very title of this contribution links the return of fascism on the political scene with the crisis of contemporary capitalism. Fascism is not synonymous with an authoritarian police regime that rejects the uncertainties of parliamentary electoral democracy. Fascism is a particular political response to the challenges with which the management of capitalist society may be confronted in specific circumstances.

## Unity and Diversity of Fascism

Political movements that can rightly be called fascist were in the forefront and exercised power in a number of European countries, particularly during the 1930s and up to 1945. These included Italy's Benito Mussolini, Germany's Adolf Hitler, Spain's Francisco Franco, Portugal's António de Oliveira Salazar, France's Philippe Pétain, Hungary's Miklós Horthy, and Romania's Ion Antonescu, Croatia's Ante Pavelić. The diversity of societies that were the victims of fascism—both major developed capitalist societies and minor dominated capitalist societies, some connected with a victorious war, others the product of defeat—should prevent us from lumping them all together. This diversity of structures and conjunctures produced different effects in these societies.

Yet, beyond this diversity, all these fascist regimes had two characteristics in common:

(i) All of these societies were willing to manage the government and society in such a way as not to call the fundamental principles of capitalism into question, specifically private capitalist property, including that of modern monopoly capitalism. Hence referring to these forms of fascism as particular ways of managing capitalism and not political forms that challenge capitalism's legitimacy, even if "capitalism" or "plutocracies" were subject to long diatribes in the rhetoric of fascist speeches. The lie that hides the true nature of these speeches appears as soon as one examines the "alternative" proposed by these various forms of fascism: private capitalist property. It remains the case that the fascist choice is not the only response to the challenges confronting the political management of a capitalist society. It is only in certain conjunctures of violent and deep crisis that the fascist solution appears to be the best one for dominant capital, or sometimes even the only possible one. The analysis must, then, focus on these crises.

(ii) The fascist choice for managing a capitalist society in crisis is always based—by definition even—on the categorical rejection of "democracy." Fascism always replaces the general principles on which the theories and practices of modern democracies are based—recognition of a diversity of opinions, recourse to electoral procedures to determine a majority, guarantee of the rights of the minority, and so on—with the opposed values of submission to the requirements of collective discipline and the authority of the supreme leader and his main agents. This reversal of values is then always accompanied by a return of backward-looking ideas, which are able to provide an apparent legitimacy to the procedures of submission that are implemented. The proclamation of the supposed necessity of returning to the (medieval) past, of submitting to state religion or to some supposed characteristic of the "race" or the (ethnic) "nation" make up the panoply of ideological discourses deployed by the fascist powers.

The diverse forms of fascism found in modern European history share these two characteristics and fall into one of the following four categories:

### 1. THE FASCISM OF THE MAJOR "DEVELOPED" CAPITALIST POWERS THAT ASPIRED TO BECOME DOMINANT HEGEMONIC POWERS IN THE WORLD, OR AT LEAST IN THE REGIONAL, CAPITALIST SYSTEM

Nazism is the model of this type of fascism. Germany became a major industrial power beginning in the 1870s and a competitor of the hegemonic powers of the era, Great Britain and France, and of the country that aspired to become hegemonic, the United States. After Germany's 1918 defeat, it had to deal with the consequences of its failure to achieve its hegemonic aspirations. Hitler clearly formulated his plan to establish over Europe, including Russia and maybe beyond, the hegemonic domination of "Germany," that is, the capitalism of the monopolies that had supported the rise of Nazism. He was disposed to accept a compromise with his major opponents: Europe and Russia would be given to him, China to Japan, the rest of Asia and Africa to Great Britain, and the Americas to the United States. His error was in thinking that such a compromise was possible: Great Britain and the United States did not accept it, while Japan, on the other hand, supported it.

Japanese fascism belongs to this same category. Since 1895, modern capitalist Japan aspired to impose its domination over all of East Asia. Here the slide was made "softly" from the "imperial" form of managing a rising national capitalism—based on apparently "liberal" institutions (an elected Diet), but in fact completely controlled by the Emperor and the aristocracy transformed by modernization—to a brutal system managed directly by the military high command. Nazi Germany made an alliance with imperial/fascist Japan, while Great Britain and the United States (after Pearl Harbor, in 1941) clashed with Tokyo, as did the resistance in China (the deficiencies of the Kuomintang being compensated for by the support of the Maoist communists).

2. THE FASCISM OF SECOND-RANK CAPITALIST POWERS

Italy's Mussolini (the inventor of fascism, including its name) is the prime example in this cateogory. Mussolinism was the response of the Italian right (the old aristocracy, the new bourgeoisie, and the middle class) to the crisis of the 1920s and the growing communist threat. But neither Italian capitalism nor its political instrument, Mussolini's fascism, had the ambition to dominate Europe, let alone the world. Despite all the boasts of the Duce about reconstructing the Roman Empire, Mussolini understood that the stability of his system rested on his alliance—as a subaltern—either with Great Britain (master of the Mediterranean) or Nazi Germany. Hesitation between the two possible alliances continued right up to the eve of the Second World War.

The fascism of Salazar and Franco belong to this same type as well. They were both dictators installed by the right and the Catholic Church in response to the dangers of republican liberals, or socialist republicans. For this reason Salazar and Franco were never ostracized for their anti-democratic violence (which was carried out under the pretext of anti-communism) by the major imperialist powers. Washington rehabilitated both of them after 1945 (Salazar was a founding member of NATO and Spain consented to U.S. military bases), followed by the European Community—guarantor by nature of the reactionary capitalist order. After the Carnation Revolution (1974) and the death of Franco (1975), these two systems joined the camp of the new low-intensity "democracies" of our era.

## 3. THE FASCISM OF DEFEATED POWERS

These regimes include France's Vichy government, as well as Belgium's Léon Degrelle and the "Flemish" pseudo-government supported by the Nazis. In France, the upper class chose "Hitler rather than the Popular Front" (see Annie Lacroix-Riz's books on this subject). This type of fascism, connected with defeat and submission to "German Europe," was forced to retreat into the background following the defeat of the Nazis. In France, it gave way to the Resistance Councils that, for a time, united Communists with other resistance fighters (Charles de Gaulle in particular). With the initiation of European construction and France's joining the Marshall Plan and NATO, the willing submission to U.S. hegemony, the further evolution of this type of fascism had to wait for the conservative right and the anti-communist, social-democratic right to break permanently with the radical left that came out of the anti-fascist and potentially anti-capitalist resistance.

## 4. FASCISM IN THE DEPENDENT SOCIETIES OF EASTERN EUROPE

We move down several degrees more when we come to examine the capitalist societies of Eastern Europe (Poland, the Baltic states, Romania, Hungary, Yugoslavia, Greece, and western Ukraine during the Polish era). We should here speak of backward and, consequently, dependent capitalism. In the interwar period, the reactionary ruling classes of these countries supported Nazi Germany. It is, nevertheless, necessary to examine on a case-by-case basis their political articulation with Hitler's project.

In Poland, the old hostility to Russian domination (Czarist Russia), which became hostility to the communist Soviet Union, encouraged by the popularity of the Catholic Papacy, would normally have made this country into Germany's vassal, on the Vichy model. But Hitler did not understand it that way: the Poles, like the Russians, Ukrainians, and Serbs, were people destined for extermination, along with Jews, the Roma, and several others. There was, then, no place for a Polish fascism allied with Berlin.

Horthy's Hungary and Antonescu's Romania were, on the other hand, treated as subaltern allies of Nazi Germany. Fascism in these two countries was itself the result of social crises specific to each of them: the fear of "communism" after the Béla Kun period in Hungary and the national chauvinist mobilization against Hungarians and Ruthenians in Romania.

In Yugoslavia, Hitler's Germany (followed by Mussolini's Italy) supported an "independent" Croatia, confided to the management of the anti-Serb Ustashi with the decisive support of the Catholic Church, while the Serbs were marked for extermination.

The Russian Revolution had obviously changed the situation with regard to the prospects of working-class struggles and the response of the reactionary propertied classes, not only on the territory of pre-1939 Soviet Union, but also in the lost territories of the Baltic states and Poland. Following the Treaty of Riga in 1921, Poland annexed the western parts of Belarus (Volhynia) and Ukraine (southern Galicia, which was previously an Austrian crownland, and northern Galicia, which had been a province of the czarist empire).

In this whole region, two camps took form from 1917 (and even from 1905, with the first Russian revolution): pro-socialist (who became pro-Bolshevik), which was popular in large parts of the peasantry (which aspired to a radical agrarian reform for their benefit) and in intellectual circles (Jews in particular); and anti-socialist (who were consequently complaisant with regard to anti-democratic governments under fascist influence), which was popular in all the landowning classes. The reintegration of the Baltic states, Belarus, and western Ukraine into the Soviet Union in 1939 emphasized this contrast.

The political map of the conflicts between pro-fascists and anti-fascists in this part of Eastern Europe was blurred, on the one hand, by the conflict between Polish chauvinism (which persisted in its project of "Polonizing" the annexed Belarusian and Ukrainian regions by settler colonies) and its victims and, on the other hand, by the conflict between the Ukrainian "nationalists," who were both anti-Polish and anti-Russian (because of anti-communism) and Hitler's project, which envisaged no Ukrainian state as a subaltern ally and simply marked its people for extermination.

Olha Ostriitchouk's authoritative work *Les Ukrainiens face à leur passé* (2013) provides a rigorous analysis of the contemporary history of this region (Austrian Galicia, Polish Ukraine, Little Russia, which became Soviet Ukraine), and provides an understanding of the issues at stake in the still ongoing conflicts as well as the place occupied by local fascism.

## THE WESTERN RIGHT'S COMPLAISANT VIEW OF PAST AND PRESENT FASCISM

The right in European parliaments between the two world wars was always complaisant about fascism and even about the more repugnant Nazism. Churchill himself, regardless of his extreme "Britishness," never hid his sympathy for Mussolini. U.S. presidents, and the establishment Democratic and Republican parties, only discovered belatedly the danger presented by Hitler's Germany and, above all, imperial/fascist Japan. With all the cynicism characteristic of the U.S. establishment, Truman openly avowed what others thought quietly: allow the war to wear out its protagonists—Germany, Soviet Russia, and the defeated Europeans—and intervene as late as possible to reap the benefits. That is not at all the expression of a principled anti-fascist position. No hesitation was shown in the rehabilitation of Salazar and Franco in 1945. Furthermore, connivance with European fascism was a constant in the policy of the Catholic Church. It would not strain credibility to describe Pius XII as a collaborator with Mussolini and Hitler.

Hitler's anti-Semitism itself aroused opprobrium only much later, when it reached the ultimate stage of its murderous insanity. The emphasis on hate for "Judeo-Bolshevism" stirred up by Hitler's speeches was common to many politicians. It was only after the defeat of Nazism that it was necessary to condemn anti-Semitism in principle. The task was made easier because the self-proclaimed heirs to the title of "victims of the Shoah" had become the Zionists of Israel, allies of Western imperialism against the Palestinians and the Arab people who, however, had never been involved in the horrors of European anti-Semitism.

Obviously, the collapse of the Nazis and Mussolini's Italy obliged rightist political forces in Western Europe (west of the "curtain") to distinguish themselves from those who—within their own groups—had been accomplices and allies of fascism. Yet fascist movements were only forced to retreat into the background and hide behind the scenes, without really disappearing.

In West Germany, in the name of "reconciliation," the local government and its patrons (the United States, and secondarily Great Britain and France) left in place nearly all those who had committed war crimes and crimes against humanity. In France, legal proceedings were initiated against the Resistance for "abusive executions for collaboration" when the Vichyists reappeared on the political scene with Antoine Pinay. In Italy, fascism became silent, but was still present in the ranks of Christian Democracy and the Catholic Church. In Spain, the "reconciliation" compromise imposed in 1980 by the European Community (which later became the European Union) purely and simply prohibited any reminder of Francoist crimes.

The support of the socialist and social-democratic parties of Western and Central Europe to the anti-communist campaigns undertaken by the conservative right shares responsibility for the later return of fascism. These parties of the "moderate" left had, however, been authentically and resolutely anti-fascist. Yet all of that was forgotten. With the conversion of these parties to social liberalism, their unconditional support for European construction, systematically devised as a guarantee for the reactionary capitalist order, and their no less unconditional submission to U.S. hegemony (through NATO, among other means), a reactionary bloc combining the classic right and the social liberals has been consolidated, one that could, if necessary, accommodate the new extreme right.

Subsequently, the rehabilitation of East European fascism was quickly undertaken beginning in 1990. All of the fascist movements of the countries concerned had been faithful allies or collaborators to varying degrees with Hitlerism. With the approaching defeat, a large number of their active leaders had been redeployed to the West and could, consequently, "surrender" to the U.S. armed forces. None of them were returned to Soviet, Yugoslav, or other governments in the new people's democracies to be tried for their crimes, which was in violation of Allied agreements. They all found refuge in the United States and Canada, and they were all pampered by the authorities for their fierce anti-communism!

In *Les Ukrainiens face à leur passé*, Ostriitchouk provides everything necessary to establish irrefutably the collusion between the objectives of U.S. policy (and behind it of Europe) and those of the local fascists of Eastern Europe (specifically, Ukraine). For example, "Professor" Dmytro Dontsov, until his death in 1975, published all his works in Canada. Dontsov's writings are not only violently anti-communist (the term "Judeo-Bolshevism" is customary with him), but also fundamentally anti-democratic. The governments of the so-called democratic states of the West supported (and even financed and organized) the "Orange Revolution" (the fascist counter-revolution) in Ukraine. And all that is continuing. Earlier, in Yugoslavia, Canada had also paved the way for the Croatian Ustashis.

The clever way in which the "moderate" media (which cannot openly acknowledge that they support avowed fascists) hide their support for these fascists is simple: they substitute the term "nationalist" for fascist. Professor Dontsov is no longer a fascist, he is a Ukrainian "nationalist," just like Marine Le Pen is no longer a fascist, but a nationalist (as *Le Monde*, for example, has written).

Are these authentic fascists really "nationalists," simply because they say so? That is doubtful. Nationalists today deserve this label only if they call into question the power of the actually dominant forces in the contemporary world, that is, that of the monopolies of the United States and Europe. These so-called "nationalists" are friends of Washington, Brussels, and NATO. Their "nationalism" amounts to chauvinistic hatred of largely innocent neighboring people who were never responsible for their misfortunes: for Ukrainians, it is Russians (and not the Czar); for Croatians, it is the Serbs; for the new extreme right in France, Austria, Switzerland, Greece, and elsewhere, it is "immigrants."

The danger represented by the collusion between major political forces in the United States (Republicans and Democrats) and Europe (the parliamentary right and the social liberals), on one side, and the fascists of the East, on the other, should not be underestimated. Hillary Clinton has set herself up as leading spokeswoman of this collusion and pushes war hysteria to the limit. Even more than George W. Bush (if that is possible), she calls for preventive war with a vengeance (and not only for repetition of the Cold War) against Russia (by even more open intervention in Ukraine, Georgia, and Moldova, among other places), against China, and against people in revolt in Asia, Africa, and Latin America. Unfortunately, this headlong flight of the United States in response to its decline could find sufficient support to allow Hillary Clinton to become the first woman president of the United States. Let's not forget what hides behind this false feminist.

Undoubtedly, the fascist danger might still appear today to be no threat to the "democratic" order in the United States and in Europe west of the old "curtain." The collusion between the classic parliamentary right and the social liberals makes it unnecessary for dominant capital to resort to the services of an extreme right that follows in the wake of the historical fascist movements. But then what should we conclude about the electoral successes of the extreme right over the last decade? Europeans are clearly also victims of the spread of generalized monopoly capitalism (Amin, 2013). We can see why, then, when confronted with collusion between the right and the so-called socialist left, they take refuge in electoral abstention or in voting for the extreme right. The responsibility of the potentially radical left is, in this context, huge: if this left had the audacity to propose real advances beyond current capitalism, it would gain the credibility that it lacks. An audacious radical left is necessary to provide the coherence that the current piecemeal protest movements and defensive struggles still lack. The "movement" could, then, reverse the social balance of power in favor of the working classes and make progressive advances possible. The successes won by the popular movements in South America are proof of that.

In the current state of things, the electoral successes of the extreme right stem from contemporary capitalism itself. These successes allow the media to throw together, with the same opprobrium, the "populists of the extreme right and those of the extreme left," obscuring the fact that the former are pro-capitalist (as the term extreme *right* demonstrates) and thus possible allies for capital, while the latter are the only potentially dangerous opponents of capital's system of power.

We observe, *mutatis mutandis*, a similar conjuncture in the United States, although its extreme right is never called fascist. The McCarthyism of yesterday, just like the Tea Party fanatics and warmongers (including Hillary Clinton) of today, openly defend "liberties"—understood as exclusively belonging to the owners and managers of monopoly capital—against "the government," which they suspect of acceding to the demands of the system's victims.

One last observation about fascist movements: they seem unable to know when and how to stop making their demands. The cult of the leader and blind obedience, the acritical and supreme valorization of pseudo-ethnic or pseudo-religious mythological constructions that convey fanaticism, and the recruitment of militias for violent actions make fascism into a force that is difficult to control. Mistakes, even beyond irrational deviations from the viewpoint of the social interests served by the fascists, are inevitable. Hitler was a truly mentally ill person, yet he could force the big capitalists who had put him in power to follow him to the end of his madness and he even gained the support of a very large portion of the population. Hitler is an extreme case, and even though Mussolini, Franco, Salazar, and Pétain were not mentally ill, a large number of their associates and henchmen did not hesitate to perpetrate criminal acts.

## FASCISM IN THE CONTEMPORARY SOUTH

The integration of Latin America into globalized capitalism in the nineteenth century was based on the exploitation of peasants who were reduced to the status of "peons" and their subjection to the savage practices of large landowners. The system of Porfiro Díaz in Mexico is a good example. The furtherance of this integration in the twentieth century produced the "modernization of poverty." The rapid rural exodus, more pronounced and occurring earlier in Latin America than in Asia and Africa, led to new forms of poverty in the contemporary urban favelas, which came to replace older forms of rural poverty. Concurrently, forms of political control of the masses were "modernized" by establishing dictatorships, abolishing electoral democracy, prohibiting parties and trade unions, and conferring on "modern" secret services all rights to arrest and torture. Clearly, these forms of political management are visibly similar to those of fascism found in the countries of dependent capitalism in eastern Europe. The dictatorships of twentieth century Latin America served the local reactionary bloc (large landowners, comprador bourgeoisie, and sometimes middle classes that benefited from this type of lumpen development), but above all, they served dominant foreign capital, specifically that of the United States, which, for this reason, supported these dictatorships up to their reversal by the recent explosion of popular movements. The power of these movements and the social and democratic advances that they have imposed exclude—at least in the short term—the return of parafascist dictatorships. But the future is uncertain: the conflict between the movement of the working classes and local and world capitalism has only begun. As with all types of fascism, the dictatorships of Latin America did not avoid mistakes, some of which were fatal to them. For example, Jorge Rafael Videla went to war over the Malvinas Islands to capitalize on Argentine national sentiment for his benefit.

Beginning in the 1980s, the lumpen development characteristic of the spread of generalized monopoly capitalism took over from the national populist systems of the Bandung era (1955–1980) in Asia and Africa (Amin, 2013). This lumpen development also produced forms akin both to the modernization of poverty and the modernization of repressive violence. The excesses of the post-Nasserist and post-Baathist systems in the Arab world provide good examples of this. We should not lump together the national populist regimes of the Bandung era and those of their successors, which jumped on the bandwagon of globalized neoliberalism, because they were both "non-democratic." The Bandung regimes, despite their autocratic political practices, benefitted from some popular legitimacy both because of their actual achievements, which benefited the majority of workers, and their anti-imperialist positions. The dictatorships that followed lost this legitimacy as soon as they accepted subjection to the globalized neoliberal model and accompanying lumpen development. Popular and national authority, although not democratic, gave way to police violence that was in service of the neoliberal, anti-popular, and anti-national project.

The recent popular uprisings, beginning in 2011, have called into question these dictatorships. But these dictatorships have only been called into question. An alternative movement will only find the means to achieve stability if it succeeds in combining the three objectives around which the revolts have been mobilized: continuation of the democratization of society and politics, progressive social advances, and the affirmation of national sovereignty.

We are still far from that. That is why there are multiple alternatives possible in the visible short term. Can there be a possible return to the national popular model of the Bandung era, maybe with a hint of democracy? What about a more pronounced crystallization of a democratic, popular, and national front, or a plunge into a backward-looking illusion that, in this context, takes on the form of an "Islamization" of politics and society?

In the conflict over these three possible responses to the challenge, the Western powers (the United States and its subaltern European allies) have made their choice: they have given preferential support to the Muslim Brotherhood and/or other "Salafist" organizations of political Islam. The reason for that is simple and obvious: these reactionary political forces accept exercising their power within globalized neoliberalism (and thus abandoning any prospect for social justice and national independence). That is the sole objective pursued by the imperialist powers.

Consequently, political Islam's program belongs to the type of fascism found in dependent societies. In fact, it shares with all forms of fascism two fundamental characteristics: (i) the absence of a challenge to the essential aspects of the capitalist order (and in this context this amounts to not challenging the model of lumpen development connected to the spread of globalized neoliberal capitalism); and (ii) the choice of anti-democratic, police-state forms of political management (such as the prohibition of parties and organizations and the forced Islamization of morals).

The anti-democratic option of the imperialist powers (which gives the lie to the pro-democratic rhetoric found in the flood of propaganda to which we are subjected), then, accepts the possible "excesses" of the Islamic regimes in question. Like other types of fascism, and for the same reasons, these excesses are inscribed in the "genes" of political Islam's modes of thought: unquestioned submission to leaders, fanatic valorization of adherence to the state religion, and the formation of shock forces used to impose submission. In fact, and this can be seen already, the "Islamist" program makes progress only in the context of a civil war (between, among others, Sunnis and Shias) and results in nothing other than permanent chaos. This type of Islamist power is, then, the guarantee that the societies in question will remain absolutely incapable of asserting themselves on the world scene. It is clear that a declining United States has given up on getting something better—a stable and submissive local government—in favor of this "second best." Similar developments and choices are found outside of the Arab-Muslim world, such as Hindu India, for example. The Bharatiya Janata Party (BJP), which just won the elections in India, is a reactionary Hindu religious party that accepts the inclusion of its government into globalized neoliberalism. It is the guarantor that India, under its government, will retreat from its project to be an emerging power. Describing it as fascist, then, is not really straining credibility too much.

In conclusion, fascism has returned to the West, East, and South; and this return is naturally connected with the spread of the systemic crisis of generalized, financialized, and globalized monopoly capitalism. Actual or even potential recourse to the services of the fascist movement by the dominant centers of this hard-pressed system calls for the greatest vigilance on our part. This crisis is destined to grow worse and, consequently, the threat of resorting to fascist solutions will become a real danger. Hillary Clinton's support for Washington's warmongering does not bode well for the immediate future.

## The Ukrainian Crisis, the Eurasian Project, and Putin's Balancing Act

The current Ukrainian crisis sheds light on the outcome to date of Russian (and, of course, Ukrainian) history. It clarifies the nature of the oligarchies that took over from the *nomenklatura* in the countries of the former Soviet Union and their savage capitalist choices (which Alexandr Buzgalin describes as "Jurassic Park capitalism"). It reveals their ambitions, the limitations of what they can accomplish, and their willingness to act as a transmission belt for the globalized domination of the financial capital of the triad's collective imperialism. But, in the case of Russia, it also reveals the possibility that they have to move in a different direction by forming closer ties to the emerging countries (Russia belongs to the so-called BRICS group). It also shows that the necessary conditions for the possible success of this venture are far from being assured. The Ukrainian crisis also reveals—this goes without saying—the true aspirations of the dominant powers of the imperialist triad and the unscrupulous means they are willing to use to achieve their ends, from the manipulation of unemployed people to the exercise of terror by fascist militias. The Ukrainian conflict is thus part of a larger context in which the strategy deployed by Washington and its subaltern European allies is coming up against the—albeit confused—aspirations of the people, nations, and even states of the contemporary periphery: Russia and the other countries of the former Soviet Union as well as those of Asia, Africa, and Latin America. The global dimensions of the questions posed by the current crises in Russia and Ukraine will be revisited later in this text.

It is certain that the United States and Europe organized a real "Euro-Nazi" putsch in Kiev in February 2014. The Western media clergy, which spouts clichés about the promise of democracy, is purely and simply lying. The powers of the triad have never promoted democracy anywhere. On the contrary, they have always supported the staunchest opponents of democracy, including fascists, who have been cleverly renamed "nationalists." In the former Yugoslavia, the Europeans supported those who were nostalgic for Croatian fascism, brought back from their Canadian exile; in Kosovo, they gave power to drug and prostitution mafias; in the Arab countries, they continue to support the most reactionary political Islam, itself financed by the new democratic republics that Saudi Arabia and Qatar will surely become. The military intervention in Iraq and Libya has destroyed these countries, without in the least promoting the promise of democracy. In Syria, the military support of the powers of the triad to the "Islamists," directly or through Saudi Arabia and Qatar, promises nothing better.

The self-proclaimed government in Kiev took the precaution of giving itself the appearance of legitimacy by holding elections. The candidates of these elections even took the precaution of not embracing the fascist militias that brought them to power. That allowed the Western media to present them as "nationalist democrats." In fact, it was an electoral farce, in the Arab World as elsewhere. The brutal repression of all resistance to the junta—the prohibition of parties considered to be "pro-Russian," a stranglehold on the media, the massacre of opponents, as in Odessa (where the justice system, which is controlled by the militias, has refrained from prosecuting the criminals who have gone after the families of victims)—has not been the subject of any commentary by the media clergy of the triad. They attribute responsibility for the Ukrainian situation solely to the excessive expansionist ambitions of Putin, who is accused of having violated the independence of the Ukrainian nation (by annexing Crimea and supporting the separatists of eastern Ukraine). This is a curious accusation coming from those who have unhesitatingly violated the independence of Serbia, Iraq, and Syria and continue to envisage the same for other countries.

The Kiev government has come up against an obstacle that is not only "ethnic" in nature, which ostensibly pits Russophones and Ukrainophones against each other. It is important to note that the borders of the republics of the former USSR had been deliberately drawn by the Soviet government to favor non-Russian nationalities in a spirit of breaking with Great Russian chauvinism. The example of Crimea, which had never been Ukrainian, is evidence of that. Donetsk and Odessa had never been "ethnically" Ukrainian. As with the Yugoslavian republics, these borders had not been drawn to become the basis for secessionist states. Putin is probably not a hero of democratic causes, but here he is only supporting those in Ukraine who reject the Euro-German colonization that Brussels wants to impose, just as it has done in eastern Europe, Greece, and Cyprus. It is not only the Russophones of Ukraine who might reject the European project, even if the despotic powers of the Kiev junta do not allow the expression of any such opposition to the Euro-German project.

Russia is searching for a place in the world system of today and tomorrow. It is now encircled by NATO forces. The threat is not the product of Putin's hallucinations. It is real and was put in place by the United States and Europe when they violated their commitment not to integrate eastern Europe, particularly the Baltic states, into NATO. Today the threat is to include Ukraine in this aggressive organization. Yet we should know by now that unkept promises are par for the course when it comes to imperialist policies (since 1492). One has to be naïve to believe the word of Washington and Brussels. This naïveté was shown again when Russia and China abstained from using their Security Council veto to deprive the attack on Libya of all legitimacy. But it seems that Moscow and Beijing have finally learned from their mistakes. In response to the expansionist project of the United States and German Europe, Putin seems to have adopted the idea of building a vast alliance of peoples from the former USSR. This alliance is now known as "Euro-Asian." This is not a recent, artificial invention. Recall that this idea responds to the centuries-long search by Russia for the definition of its place in the world. Why should this right be refused to Russians and other peoples of the former USSR?

Moscow's fight against the imperialist order, in Ukraine and elsewhere, will be victorious only if the people involved resolutely support it. This support, in turn, will be possible only if Russia frees itself from the shackles of neoliberalism, the origin of social disaster, in Russia as elsewhere. Up to now, Putin has carried out a perilous balancing act in his attempt to continue a disastrous internal neo-liberal policy, on the one hand, and to defend the legitimate interests of an independent Russia on the other. Abandoning neoliberalism and escaping from financial globalization are now both necessary and possible. This imperative applies not only to Russia, but also to the BRICS and all the countries of the global South. There are still today segments of the political class in Russia that are disposed to support a state capitalism that would, in turn, be open to the possibility of moving in the direction of a democratic and socialized management. But if the comprador fraction of the Russian ruling classes—the exclusive beneficiaries of neoliberalism—ends up gaining the upper hand, then the "sanctions" with which Europe is intimidating Russia could bear fruit. The comprador segments are still disposed to capitulate to preserve their portion of the spoils from the pillaging of their country. Russia then would not be able to reject colonization by the imperialism of the triad. And in the meantime, Russia will lose the battle in Ukraine.

## REFERENCES

Amin, Samir, *The Implosion of Contemporary Capitalism*, (New York: Monthly Review Press, 2013).

Ostrutchouk, Olha, *Les Ukrainiens face à leur passé* [Ukrainians Faced with Their Past], (Brussels: P. I. E. Lang, 2013).

# Assessment and Perspectives

There is one global history. However, there are different views of that global history. The history of a particular region of the world (in this case, Russia) acquires meaning only when placed within global history as conceived by a particular author. I explained my perspective in my book *Global History: A View from the South*: (i) my view is inspired by Marx's historical materialism, but I keep my distance from the historical Marxisms of the various Internationals; and (ii) my view is inseparable from my standpoint as an activist, both internationalist and universalist, for the liberation of the peoples of the periphery from the globalized capitalist system through a socialist surpassing of capitalism.

Yet global history presents dangerous traps for its defenders. The first of them is to fall into a philosophy of history that, far from being derived from the actual history as conceptualized by the author in question, is in fact the point of departure, conceived in an *a priori* way. Henri Pirenne is one example. For the entire history of humanity, Pirenne counterposes maritime worlds, which are open, democratic, and described as capitalist, to continental worlds, which are closed, despotic, and described as feudal. This *a priori* view, which is without any scientific value, despite the more than respectable erudition of the author, has become the currently fashionable ideology. In this perspective, the world of the Atlantic and the Pacific—in practical terms, the triad of the United States, Europe, and Japan—is the world of the efficient (so-called market) economy, democracy, and peace. It is colliding with the excessive ambitions of the continental worlds—Russia, China, and the Arab and Muslim world—which are inevitably despotic and aggressive.

The second trap, always connected to the first, is to succumb to attempts at articulating an ahistorical perspective in which history repeats similar cycles. This perspective does not take into account the qualitative differences between the important stages of history. Paul Kennedy's ahistorical theory of the expansion and decline of empires comes to mind as an example of this. For my part, I have refused to blur the distinction between pre-capitalist global history, which is structured around societies based on what I have called a tributary mode of production (in its various guises), and the history of modern times, which is based on the mode of production of historical capitalism beginning in 1800.

The third trap is amateurism. Global history requires the work of scholars, whose erudition is not academic finery, but the expression of the field's requirements. I am not an historian by trade, but only a reader—an attentive reader, I believe—of the works of professional historians. It is up to the reader to judge the quality of what I am offering here: Is this work a study supported by the works of historians of Russia or a quick essay by an amateur?

I now come to the conclusions that I have drawn from my reading of the history of Russia. These conclusions concern the past, on the one hand, and the present and possible future, on the other.

As for the more distant past, as previously noted, the formation of the Russian state does not appear to be different from the formation of the kingdoms of France and Great Britain, for example. This occurred in a time period prior to capitalist modernity. Of course, national popular historians prefer to paint a rosy picture of the formation of their modern nation, without necessarily taking a dark view of the formation of other nations. Looking back from the present, it is possible, however, to judge this past with more severity. An honest Frenchman or Frenchwoman acknowledges the horrors of the Albigensian Crusade, without which the later—and slow—merging of France and Occitania would have been impossible; an honest Briton acknowledges the horrors of the colonization of Ireland; an honest Russian acknowledges the horrors of Czarist despotism (and the Bolsheviks, for good class reasons, painted the blackest picture of it possible). For my part, I have emphasized the resemblance and analogy of these three national constructions; whether one gives a positive or negative coloration to the events involved is a personal decision. While the constructions of France and Great Britain are attributed to their kings and that of Russia to its emperor (czar), the distinction in titles has no significance. Kings are monarchs of geographically limited spaces, while the king of the gigantic Russian space becomes emperor.

For the less distant past, on the other hand, the difference between the construction of the colonial empires and that of the czarist empire should be emphasized. The former were inseparable from the development of capitalism whereas the latter had little to do with it (except perhaps from the end of the nineteenth century). In this sense, it would be more accurate to compare the construction of the Russian Empire with that of the Ottoman Empire or the Chinese Empire

Conclusions concerning the present and visible future should be placed within a completely different and new context. My interpretation of the global history of the capitalist era focuses on the systematic construction of the center-periphery polarization, followed by the completion of the conquest of the Earth by the historical imperialisms of the centers (European, U.S., and Japanese) in the nineteenth century and the first wave of victorious struggles by the peripheries in the twentieth century, which—partially—freed themselves from imperialist domination (or, more precisely, forced the imperialist powers to adjust to the advances of the peripheries toward their liberation). The history of the Soviet Union should be viewed within this context. The first awakening of the South (also the title of one of my books) ended between 1980 and 1990 and was followed by the beginning of the current situation, which is characterized by the offensive of the new collective imperialism of the triad to reestablish its domination of the world, on the one hand, and the rise of a second wave of resistance in an awakening of the peripheries, on the other.

This is a dramatic moment. The new imperialism is still on the offensive, even if it is running out of steam and getting bogged down in conflicts that it has been unable to control, as Michel Raimbaud (2015) demonstrates. The offensive against Russia, begun with the attempt to colonize Ukraine, is at its height. It is not the only one. The conflict with the major emerging power, China, is latent. The offensive of the United States and its subaltern European allies requires the systematic destruction of the Arab world, Iran, and, beyond that, the Muslim world of Asia and sub-Saharan Africa. Archaic and reactionary political Islam, inspired by the Arab countries of the Persian Gulf (privileged allies of the West), is the instrument being used. The chaos connected with the regression of the societies in question in effect guarantees their inability to become positive actors in the transformation of the world.

The stakes in this battle are immense: Who will win? Will it be collective imperialism, which is leading the entire planet to self-destruction (ecological, among other types) by establishing a system of apartheid on the world scale (involving genocide when necessary)? Or will the second awakening of the South force the imperialist North to retreat, thereby opening the door to a possible coming together between the struggles of people in the peripheries and struggles that the workers in the North could be on the verge of undertaking? To which of these two camps will Russia commit itself? The Russia of the 1990s experienced the illusion of its adoption by the triad, particularly through the actions of its European partner. Gorbachev's naïve project of the "common European house" was based on this illusion. Europe (mainly Germany, Great Britain, and France) did not and does not want that. Europe has its eyes set on its "Latin America" in a reconquered eastern Europe. It has the ambition, with and behind the United States, of colonizing Russia, beginning with Ukraine.

Putin's Russia seems to have become aware of the real objectives of Washington and Brussels. Nevertheless, Putin has not (or not yet) completely left behind the confusion of the post-Soviet period. He remains a partisan of the "market economy" understood as synonymous with the management of the local production system by financialized monopolies, in which the local oligarchy (in Russia as in Europe and the United States) is the managing political force. He remains a conservative motivated by confused rightist thought, as Michel Eltchaninoff (2015) demonstrates. I have already expressed my opinion on this contradiction: without loosening the connection to this type of economic and social management, it is impossible to move forward with the project of sovereign development, sheltered from Western aggression. This observation is valid, beyond Russia, for all emergent countries except maybe, and up to a certain point, China.

An assessment of the history of Russia in the long run is, consequently, difficult to make today. History in the long run is not a peacefully flowing river, but made up of different moments, separated by tumultuous rapids. The present conjuncture, open to all possible futures, from the best to the worst, makes it impossible to see the visible short term clearly.

## REFERENCES

Amin, Samir, *Global History: A View From the South,* (Oxford: Pambazuka, 2011).

Eltchaninoff, Michel, *Dans la tête de Vladimir Poutine* [Inside Vladimir Putin's Head], (Arles, France: Actes Sud-Solin, 2015).

Raimbaud, Michel, *Tempête sur le Grand Moyen-Orient* [Storm over the Greater Middle East], (Paris: Ellipses, 2015).

# Index